Executive Function Essentials in the Classroom

from the author

Raising an ADHD Child
A Handbook for Parents of Distractible, Dreamy and Defiant Children
Fin O'Regan and Zoe Beezer
Illustrated by Richard Johnston
ISBN 978 1 83997 021 4
eISBN 978 1 83997 022 1

Executive Function Essentials in the Classroom

Strategies to Support Learning and Growth

Zoe Beezer

Jessica Kingsley Publishers
London and Philadelphia

First published in Great Britain in 2025 by Jessica Kingsley Publishers
An imprint of John Murray Press

1

A CIP catalogue record for this title is available from the
British Library and the Library of Congress

ISBN 978 1 80501 077 7
eISBN 978 1 80501 081 4

Printed and bound in Great Britain by Clays Ltd

Jessica Kingsley Publishers' policy is to use papers that are natural,
renewable and recyclable products and made from wood grown in
sustainable forests. The logging and manufacturing processes are expected
to conform to the environmental regulations of the country of origin.

Jessica Kingsley Publishers
Carmelite House
50 Victoria Embankment
London EC4Y 0DZ

www.jkp.com

John Murray Press
Part of Hodder & Stoughton Limited
An Hachette UK Company

The authorised representative in the EEA is Hachette Ireland,
8 Castlecourt Centre, Dublin 15, D15 XTP3, Ireland (email: info@hbgi.ie)

Contents

Introduction 7

Part 1: Executive Functioning Skills Basics and Essentials

1. What Are Executive Function Skills? 15

2. The Science Behind Executive Functioning and How to
   Improve Them. 23

3. How to Be an Effective Teacher of Executive Function Skills . 27

4. Neurodiversity, Developmental Differences and Executive
   Function Skills. 45

Part 2: Specific Executive Function Skills

5. Response Inhibition 53

6. Emotional Control 63

7. Flexibility. 75

8. Task Initiation. 85

9. Sustained Attention 97

10. Goal-Directed Persistence 107

11. Planning and Prioritisation 121

12. Organisation. 129

13. Time Management 135

14. Working Memory. 147

15. Metacognition. 159

Part 3: Awareness and Home Environment

16. How Parents Can Help to Support and Hone Executive
Function Skills. 179

Bibliography 215

Introduction

Aim of this book

Executive function (EF) skills are an interrelated set of mental processes that control our thoughts, actions and emotions; the core EF skills are working memory, inhibitory control and cognitive flexibility. Underdeveloped EF skills can affect an individual's response inhibition, working memory, emotional control, sustained attention, task initiation, planning and prioritising, time management, goal-directed persistence, flexible thinking and metacognition.

The aim of this book is to explain and explore how challenges with EF skills can impact learning and classroom performance, and to provide suggestions and strategies to support pupils within mainstream education. It will provide teachers with resources that they can employ with minimal impact to their workload and with little sacrifice to curriculum teaching time.

While this book is primarily geared towards educators, poor executive functioning affects all parts of an individual's life, and therefore parents and caregivers[1] may also find it useful – indeed, most of the strategies suggested are transferable to the home environment.

Without doubt the world that we inhabit has changed enormously from that even of our parents – the advent of the internet, mobile phones, social media and gaming (to name just a few of the advances in technology) means that a child and teenager's environment is more distracting, stimulating and demanding than it has ever been before. We are also a society that, in our ancestors' terms, have far more possessions

---

1   When referring to 'parents' throughout the book, I am referring to all caregivers.

to take care of. This means that young people have more potential for distraction, but there is an increased need for organisation!

The aim of this book is to show you how, without increasing your workload dramatically, but with some minor adaptations to your teaching routines, you can improve EF awareness and productivity within your class, and thereby help the young people in your care to become more autonomous and independent learners. Poor executive functioning can affect anyone, including those individuals who are very capable and who can handle high-level content and higher-order thinking skills, and who may not typically be associated with needing 'help', but who may not be able to manage some of the day-to-day functional demands that are placed on them. Everyone will benefit, no one will be disadvantaged by it, and for some, it will be transformational!

This book is aimed at all those students (and adults!) who may have trouble with (to name just a few of the challenges):

- Deadlines

- Files and paperwork

- Timetables and agendas

- Managing the school day

- Disorganisation

- Forgetfulness

- Getting started on tasks

- Emotional control.

All these difficulties (and more) fall under the umbrella of poor EF skills.

The prefrontal cortex, the part of the brain that controls executive function, is where our most advanced thinking takes place, and it continues to develop until our mid-twenties. This means that there are years of opportunity during a child's school life to really help develop their EF skills. If we do this alongside instilling an understanding that cognition and ability are not preordained and fixed, but continue to develop and grow, then the 'education years' should be a truly exciting time to be part of an individual's development! By teaching pupils to be open-minded to learning, and by incorporating EF awareness into their daily lives, we can have an impact on young lives that extends far beyond the school environment, and which will be life-long and life-enhancing!

How to use this book

Whether you choose to read this book from cover to cover, or you dip in and out of it, it is important to remember that different EFs develop at different ages and stages in a child and young adult's life, and these skills usually naturally improve as they get older. You will need to bear in mind the age of the individual when considering the strategies to use, and how independent they should be in the development of their EF skills.

The reason the book is designed to be picked up and put down, and dipped in and out of, is to encourage you to get started with implementing EF awareness in the young people in your care, no matter how small you start. It does not need to be a programme of change that feels daunting or overwhelming – therefore you are encouraged to access the suggestions in this book at the pace and level that works for you. To minimise the amount of reading needed to get started, this book has limited examples, anecdotes and interesting and entertaining accounts of EFs in practice, so that you can access what you need to, as efficiently as you need to. Having said that, if you are able to read each of these pared-back chapters from cover to cover, then you will, of course, develop a far greater understanding of EFs, and you will be much more likely to instinctively be able to identify core EF strengths and weaknesses among your pupils, and be better equipped to meet their needs.

If this book piques your interest to explore EFs in greater detail, there are several excellent books on the market to help you do that (see, for example, Guare, Dawson and Guare 2009; Guare, Dawson and Guare 2013; Moyes 2014).

Teaching EF skills

A positive, proactive and consistent approach, with good role modelling, will encourage students to develop habits and expertise through repetition and practice.

Each opportunity to practise and strengthen EFs will ultimately result in a decreased load placed on the brain, because healthy EF habits will become far more automatic the more they are practised. This, in turn, will enable pupils to have more brain functioning capacity to focus on the teaching and learning aspects of their education. As teachers, we need to convey to students the message that for all of us (even 'us'), taking small steps and knowing that *practice makes perfect* is the key to success.

When considering how you might implement some EF changes and use some of the strategies suggested in this book, it is worth holding in mind that Albert Mehrabian defined communication as follows:

- 7% words

- 38% tonality, volume and tempo

- 55% non-verbal signals.[2]

In other words, most communication is not about words, but rather, how those words are delivered. As a teacher, you already know the importance of delivery and how to keep students actively listening and engaged. It is important to remember the verbal and non-verbal signals the pupils pick up on. When dealing with students' EF vulnerabilities you will need to appear interested and focused on supporting them, employ active listening skills, and be mindful of facial expressions and body language when students inevitably experience their own hiccups and weaknesses.

Also, as you work through this book, it is important to model to the student how to self-reflect and learn from setbacks. Instil in them an understanding that those strategies that did not work are just setbacks to be learned from, and not failures. Initially this will require explicit conversations with pupils about what was successful and what was not, until they become practised at this, and the dialogue can transfer from the explicit teacher to pupil to becoming internalised self-talk.

It is also important to remember that while you can help to improve the EF skills of all the pupils you teach, some may have complex EF needs and may need additional input beyond the classroom to truly support them. Even so, the scaffolding that you provide within the classroom will still be hugely beneficial to them.

---

2   See https://worldofwork.io/2019/07/mehrabians-7-38-55-communication-model

The scope of this book

In this book we will also take a brief look at other factors that affect a pupil's day and their learning but that do not necessarily fall under the remit of EF skills but are very closely linked. For example, mindset or stress levels can interfere with our ability to learn – and so you will find some sections that deviate from explicitly addressing EFs, and that explore complementary skills for growth mindset (Dweck 2017), stress management, exercise and mood management.

How this book is structured

- Part 1 of this book includes the first four chapters, which are designed to provide you with some essential basics about EF skills so that you understand what they are, why they are so important, and how they develop.

- Part 2 (Chapters 5–15) explores each of the individual EF skills in more detail, providing strategies and interventions.

- Part 3 (Chapter 16) focuses on involving parents in raising EF awareness at school and in the home environment, with some guides for parents provided.

The resources are found wherever you see the symbol █ and can be downloaded from https://digitalhub.jkp.com/redeem using the code UNPVSWJ.

PART 1

EXECUTIVE FUNCTIONING SKILLS

Basics and Essentials

CHAPTER 1

What Are Executive Function Skills?

What are EF skills?

Executive functions are a group of complex mental processes and cognitive abilities required to plan and direct activities and help us to regulate our behaviour. They enable us to self-reflect and think flexibly, set goals, and complete them efficiently and effectively. They help us to balance, analyse and prioritise our demands and desires such as our wants, needs and 'have to' haves. They are like the CEO of a company, the conductor of an orchestra, or an air traffic controller at an airport ensuring that takeoff and landing happens in a smooth and coordinated manner.

EF skills are housed in the prefrontal cortex of the brain and begin to develop from birth but do not reach maturity until into someone's mid-twenties! There is therefore enormous scope to help the lives of pupils run more smoothly and to free up more time and energy for learning, by supporting their EF development. Adults can also continue to work on improving EF skills – although it requires effort to create new habits, it is possible!

Recognising the traits and characteristics of executive dysfunction

EF challenges at school include:

- Meltdowns (response inhibition / emotional control).

- During the normal school day, pupils receiving a lot of discrete assistance from members of the school community (with task initiation, planning and prioritisation, organisation, time management) to help them 'keep on track'; when this scaffolding is not there, they may find it more difficult to organise themselves – homework might not get done, get handed in late or be frequently lost.

- Low self-awareness and poor ability to self-monitor and to problem solve (metacognition).

- Difficulty moving between 'lessons' or dealing with unexpected changes to the day (flexibility).

- Difficulty maintaining a level of engagement, especially for subjects / tasks deemed 'less interesting' (sustained attention).

- Struggling to retain information or instructions while performing tasks (working memory).

- Difficulty pursuing and completing a task (goal-directed persistence).

For these pupils, no matter how hard they try to overcome these difficulties, a new scenario always occurs.

Everyone has EF strengths and weaknesses, and the more someone understands about their own EF profile, the more they can take advantage of their natural strengths and strengthen their weaker skills. It is probably fair to say that at some point most pupils will have had struggles with emotional control and friendships, or with organisational skills and the ability to prioritise and execute important (but perhaps undesirable) jobs or tasks. Indeed, we can also probably self-reflect and identify with some of these challenges at some point in our own lives.

You can probably recall and bring to mind pupils (or classes!) who seem to persistently struggle with the mechanics of being in your class – they may well have good subject knowledge, but somehow do not use their time productively to execute tasks and to demonstrate their ability. There are also those pupils who fly slightly under your radar, who are doing okay, but who might not be performing perhaps as well as they could. These groups of pupils are not yet independent learners and are at risk of failing to meet their potential.

It should also be noted that pupils with additional needs often have particular EF challenges because of the extra demands on them and the extra effort they must put into their day, which means that they find it hard to juggle everything.

From this, you can see how addressing EF needs within the classroom might have an impact on a sizeable number of pupils. And for those others in the class who do not readily fall into these categories, even for them, out of the list of 11 EFs there will almost certainly be areas where improvements in their skills will help them to function even more successfully within school and in life more generally.

EF definitions

Over the course of this book each of the individual EF skills will be expanded on in separate chapters dedicated to the key skillset. No one EF skill can work in isolation, and they are often interconnected, meaning that all need to be working together to get optimal output – much the same as individual instruments playing together in harmony in an orchestra.

EF skill	Definition	Examples of EF challenges
Response inhibition	Self-restraint, the capacity to think before you act, the ability to resist the urge to say or do something, allowing you time to evaluate the situation and how your behaviour may have an impact	• Acting before you think • Not thinking about the consequences • Blurting out answers / thoughts and not being able to wait until asked
Emotional control	The ability to regulate your emotions The ability to conduct healthy personal and school-based relationships	• Getting easily frustrated • Getting stressed • Getting easily upset • Arguing back with the teacher / pupils • Finding it hard to control exuberance in class / with peers

EF skill	Definition	Examples of EF challenges
Flexibility	The ability to be adaptable and to be willing to change plans and direction, where needed	• Finding it hard to 'go with the flow' • Finding it hard when plans change • Getting upset if things don't go according to plan • Difficulty switching easily between tasks / moving between lesson topics – wanting to finish a previous task and finding it hard to move on
Task initiation	The ability to start tasks without putting them off	• Finding it hard to stop doing something that interests you in order to prioritise work (playing online games, social media etc.) • Finding it hard to get straight on with tasks set by the teacher – requiring input to get started or using strategies (sharpening pencils, going to the loo, filling a water bottle) to put off starting
Sustained attention	The ability to focus and pay attention, even if the task is not very engaging	• Difficulty following through and being able to complete a task without supervision or external pressure to complete it • Starting something and not finishing it • In class finding it hard to work for the required period without distraction
Goal-directed persistence	The ability to meet targets and goals, by sticking at it until finished	• Difficulty with persisting at something • Giving up on things • Finding it hard to complete a project / persist with revision

Planning and prioritisation	The ability to plan how to achieve a desired goal / outcome and to prioritise the steps needed to achieve it	• Difficulty knowing how / where to start on a task • Difficulty in having an idea of the steps you need to go through to complete a project • Not knowing how to plan an essay
Organisation	The ability to have a well-ordered mind and to be neat, tidy and methodical with possessions and workspaces	• Messy, chaotic school bag • Disorganised notes • Difficulty finding things
Time management	The ability to understand the passage of time and an awareness of how long something will take Being aware of submission dates and deadlines	• Lack of punctuality, e.g., getting to lessons on time • Difficulty finishing schoolwork in a timely manner • Difficulty maintaining routines and deadlines • Difficulty working out how long something will take • Missing dates and deadlines
Working memory	The ability to hold something in mind while you perform complex tasks. It includes the ability to use past experiences to apply now or in the future Working memory consists of visual (or non-verbal) recall and verbal (or language-based) recall	• Difficulty keeping track of possessions and where you have put them • Difficulty remembering what you have to do • Not learning from past experiences • Difficulty following classroom instructions • Finding it hard to hold maths problems / essay structures etc. in mind to successfully complete them
Metacognition	The ability to be self-aware: of your skills as a learner and how you respond to events – taking a bird's eye look at yourself	• Difficulty with understanding your own learning behaviour and your own learning journey • Difficulty planning, evaluating and regulating your thoughts • Your own understanding of yourself – 'I have difficulty learning times tables / spellings' etc.

It is perfectly normal to be better at some EF skills than others. All of us at some point may struggle to be organised, resist temptation to say or do things, control our emotions, start tasks in a timely manner, plan and decide what we need to do, prioritise the important (but perhaps less engaging) things over the more interesting things, sustain our attention to complete the task even if it is boring, manage our time well, be flexible and take change in our stride, or hold information in our memory while doing a task.

It becomes harder when some or all of these difficulties are sufficiently challenging for an individual that they begin to negatively impact their life. Children and adolescents can learn to make improvements, however, because, as already identified, the prefrontal cortex, which controls these skills, is still developing, and therefore their EF skills can be improved. This means that the adults and the systems around the child must try to stop organising and problem solving for the child, and instead encourage them to pursue mastery themselves – in other words, we need to stop trying to be the child's prefrontal cortex and encourage them to develop their own EF skills. The frontal lobes of the brain (the prefrontal cortex) need to be trained to become the 'executives in charge', and teachers should scaffold and coach pupils to improve and become more autonomous in their EF awareness.

Efficient executive functioning can perhaps be likened to learning to swim – some of us take to it easily and learn quickly, whereas for others the process is more arduous and takes longer, requiring more instruction; and a small number may require buoyancy aids and to stay in the shallow end longer than expected. However, once we know how to do it, it becomes an automatic skill that we do not forget, and which requires far less investment of effort than it did when we were mastering it. In other words, it is effortless when we know how to do it, but we need to learn and practise in order to get better, and some will find this much easier than others.

Categorising EF skills

Guare, Dawson and Guare (2013), in their *Smart But Scattered* books, have separated the different EF skills into those that help to regulate our emotions (behaviour) and those that help us to think and plan (cognition).

For the purposes of this book, these categories have been redefined slightly to perhaps make them easier to understand in a classroom context. I therefore suggest that EF skills can be split into two subsets: one that revolves around how students act and engage with tasks, and one that is concerned with how they reason and problem solve.

For pupils who have more pronounced EF challenges than many of their peers, you may want to understand more about their specific areas of challenge, so that you can help to give them more focused support. By observing them you might be able to categorise some of their vulnerabilities into either difficulties with how well they are able to act and engage in class, or their problem-solving and task performance skills, and by so doing you will be able to understand more clearly the areas that they need to develop to realise their potential.

Inevitably the two sets of skills are interlinked, but you may find pupils have strengths in one area and greater areas of vulnerability in another. Therefore, if a pupil shows an ability to evaluate and problem solve to successfully perform tasks, they need to be able to manage and control their engagement in order to successfully achieve their targets and goals. Conversely, a pupil may have good skills to manage their behavioural responses, but have less well developed thinking skills to orchestrate the task.

Here are the different EF skills split into the two categories:

EF skills involving reasoning and problem solving	EF skills linked to how students act and engage with tasks
Planning and prioritisation	Response inhibition
Organisation	Emotional control
Time management	Flexibility
Working memory	Task initiation
Metacognition	Sustained attention
	Goal-directed persistence

Source: Based on Guare, Dawson and Guare (2013, p.19)

Examples of some of the different skills associated with cognition and behaviour and how they may manifest themselves within the classroom environment include the following:

How do EF skills involving reasoning and problem solving affect learning?	How do EF skills involving actions and engagement affect learning?
Making plans	Waiting to speak until you are called upon
Being able to meaningfully include past knowledge in discussions / work	Being able to change your mind and adapt to the new development while thinking, reading or writing
Evaluating ideas and reflecting on work	
Keeping track of more than one thing at once	Engaging in group dynamics
Keeping track of time and finishing work on time	Asking for help or seeking more information when needed

This overview of the individual EF skills, the explanations about *how* they can be categorised and how they can affect not only learning but also the social and emotional welfare of a pupil, has highlighted the key role EF skills play in everyday life, both inside and outside the classroom.

The following chapter extends the concept of *why* EF skills are so important, by exploring the science behind them. An understanding of this will help you to support and develop pupils' EF skills more fully.

CHAPTER 2

The Science Behind Executive Functioning and How to Improve Them

EF development

In order to understand the extraordinary value of promoting and supporting EF development in pupils it is necessary to have some understanding of brain functioning, because in so doing you will understand more clearly *what* to do, and *why* you are doing it.

An incredible period of brain growth occurs from birth to early adolescence. The back of the brain starts to develop first, and the very last bit of the brain, the prefrontal cortex, housed in the front of the brain behind the forehead, is the last to mature, continuing to develop well into a person's twenties; it is here where the EF skillset is housed and controlled.

There is a developmental timetable for the acquisition of EFs; they do not all develop in one go, but rather, they evolve and become more established in a sequential order, beginning at around age two, and not reaching full maturity until adulthood. One skill typically tends to develop on top of the other, to the point where there is interplay and interaction between all 11 EF skills.

Because of the brain's plasticity, the more an EF skill is practised, the more it is reinforced and established, until it becomes second nature. Therefore, from young children through to adults in their twenties, there is an optimal opportunity to influence and develop positive executive functioning. Beyond that age, enhancing and developing EF skills requires more conscious effort!

The science behind this is not only fascinating but also key to appreciating the power that educators have in influencing this growth.

The human brain

The central nervous system is made up of two parts: the brain and the spinal cord. Each has a distinct role – the brain acts as the control centre, and the spinal cord consists of a highway of neurons along which information is conducted from the brain to the relevant target.

Within the brain there are billions of **neurons**, each with the possibility of making connections (known as **synapses**) with other nerve cells, to form a communication network to transmit and receive information.

Each one of those neurons has three parts to it:

- A **soma**, which is the *cell body* and contains the nucleus.

- An **axon**, whose role it is to *transmit* messages and information to other neurons.

- **Dendrites**, which are like branches, *receiving* information from other neurons and sending the message to the soma.

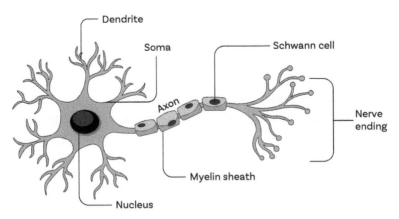

Structure of neuron

Information is transmitted between the neurons via an electrical charge that moves down the axon. The neurons communicate with each other at the point where the axons and dendrites meet, but they do not touch each other, so when the signal reaches the end of the axon, a **synapse** is formed, and neurotransmitters bridge the gap between them, to allow the 'message' to be transmitted to another neuron. Therefore, the synapse is the point of communication between two nerves. To make the speed of communication between the neurons as efficient as possible, the axons are coated in a fatty layer, which acts like an insulator and stops the electrical signal from shorting out, ensuring it is transmitted effectively – this fatty coating is called the **myelin sheath.**

The more a message is transmitted through an axon, the more the myelin sheath builds up along that axon, meaning that the transmission of information *speeds up* and allows the nerve cells to communicate more effectively with each other. The thicker the myelin coating, the faster the message transmission, and the stronger the connections between the nerve cells become. It is said to take 60+ iterations to embed new habits in the long-term memory and for them to become automatic. The saying 'practice makes perfect' is understandable in this context.

Conversely, and importantly, unused neurons and synapses are *pruned* and wither away due to inactivity. Therefore, skills can be lost if they are not used and practised. This highlights that the 'use it or lose it' slogan really applies to EF.

The chapters in Part 2 on each of the 11 individual EF skills will explore how to 'use it', so that key opportunities are not missed and a 'lose it' outcome for pupils is avoided. If we can provide pupils with rich EF learning experiences, their skills will strengthen!

CHAPTER 3

How to Be an Effective Teacher of Executive Function Skills

What do classroom teachers need to know about their own EF skills?

The best approach that a teacher can take is to create an environment where explicit reference to and reinforcement of the various EF skills is the norm. Modelling and highlighting examples of good EF functioning, as well as acknowledging situations when some EF skills are working less well, will mean that an awareness and language around EF skills will become embedded in the class culture. If you can take the additional step to model your own EF strengths and weaknesses to your pupils, they will understand that you also have your own personal strengths and challenges. If you can acknowledge when you have displayed an EF weakness and can appear relaxed about it with a growth mindset about improvement, you will be embodying the very message and learning point that you are trying to instil in your pupils. This will enable them to see that everyone has EF strengths and weaknesses, and that everyone can have good EF days and less good EF days. It will also help you to build rapport with the pupils.

The chapters in Part 2 on each of the individual EF skills provide ways to explicitly coach pupils in those specific skills. An EF skills as well as an EF-friendly classroom checklist is provided at the end of this chapter, which can help you get a broad view of your own classroom-based EF skillset and what pupils might experience when you teach them. The EF skills checklist can be used or adapted to suit students too, perhaps as an 'audit' of how they currently perceive themselves. Reviewing and redoing these 'audits' as you develop classroom awareness of EF skills could provide you with interesting qualitative tracking data, to help assess whether pupils' views of themselves as individuals and as learners changes over time.

EF in the classroom

Improving EF awareness in pupils, and adopting EF strategies to support your pupils, should also have a positive impact on you as the teacher – it should help make your class run more smoothly, allowing pupils more time to maximise their learning. Also, helping students to be more self-aware, and showing them that there are choices that they themselves can make, will help them to feel more engaged and active in their education.

Inevitably the best outcomes for the pupils would be if the whole school was involved in the process of raising awareness of and supporting EF skills – becoming part of the school language, in assemblies, form time, and even from lunchtime staff. However, if you are starting this exploration of EF skills in your own classroom, it *will* have a positive effect – and for some, it could be profound.

Probably the best approach, as you work through this book, is to consider having an *EF skill of the week* or a *half-termly EF focus*, where just one skill is focused on and developed, before building on it and introducing the next. It will enable you to see if it is making a positive impact on pupils, and it allows time for the skill to develop and embed. Remember that you need to keep on practising each of the skills so that they become automatic; therefore, once one skill has been introduced and practised, you should still keep promoting it and monitoring it as you layer on the next skill.

As teachers, we often like ways to track success, and although EF skills could be considered 'soft skills' that are hard to measure, you can still get an understanding of how pupils are developing their EF awareness by spending a few minutes getting feedback using tools such as a Mentimeter[1]

---

[1]   Interactive polls that pupils can take part in which would require pupils to have access to their mobile phone.

or Plickers,[2] or using self-reflection worksheets at the beginning and end of the half-term / term / academic year.

The importance of emotional stability

A sense of connection and belonging within the class will reduce a pupil's anxiety and help create an optimal learning environment. To understand why this is key to learning it is useful to understand about human beings' primitive fight, flight or freeze responses to anxiety, because this will influence a pupil's acquisition of new knowledge – including EF development.

For some children, stress from home or school can trigger an anxious response, which, in turn, engages the reptilian part of the brain, sending them into a fight, flight or freeze mode. This means that an automatic sense of self-preservation takes over from the rational thinking brain and prepares the body for fight, flight or freeze in anticipation of danger. In this scenario the reptilian brain overrides the prefrontal cortex, where EF skills and higher-order thinking skills occur, making it far more difficult for the individual to engage in rational thinking. When the danger is perceived to have passed, it takes the pupil a disproportionate length of time to go from a state of arousal, dysregulation and distress to a calmer state, to where they can function normally – and this is wasted learning time.

Inevitably, pupils will bring stresses from other classes / teachers, peer interactions or home into your classroom, or they may even be triggered within your class. The key clearly, therefore, is to make the school environment as non-threatening as possible, so that pupils feel well supported when they are anxious or make errors. This will limit the length of time that they might feel anxious or distressed to allow optimum learning to occur.

Often children who experience EF challenges or weaknesses are the ones in class who might draw attention to themselves and may come across as forgetful, disorganised and lazy; they may even be labelled, consciously or subconsciously in your mind, as 'naughty'. At some point

---

2 An interactive tool where pupils can be set questions or polls by the teacher; they use free printable cards to respond and teachers scan the pupils' answers to create a poll or tally of responses on their interactive whiteboards.

these children may become involved in the school's sanctions policy: academic sanctions if they persistently fail to hand in work or complete work in class; alternatively (or in addition) they might trigger the behavioural policy sanctions. This can disengage some students and make others fear the repercussions of their 'misdemeanours'.

Whatever their external reaction is to a series of class-based reprimands (e.g., a teacher calling them out publicly for *once again* failing to do something), or worse, leadership reprimands, internally they will be feeling shame and fear, and may go into fight, flight or freeze mode, which will compound their challenges – thereby preventing their reasoning brain, and their EF skills, from helping them to manage the situation. Some may react by being triggered into a fight response because of the shame and humiliation they feel, some might try to escape or avoid the situation, while others might freeze and shut down and find it hard to engage. Most pupils will try their best to live up to your expectations and outwardly seem to be doing so, but internally some may be in a state of constant anxiety for fear they will somehow let themselves, or you, down once again.

It is important, therefore, to try to minimise the anxiety levels within individual classrooms and within the school generally by fostering and promoting a supportive environment in which a growth mindset is promoted and mistakes are seen as part of learning development. When identifying 'errors' or misdemeanours, we should strive to do this in such a way that the pupil does not feel shame, but instead understands how to improve, and feels encouraged to do so.

Growth mindset and overcoming obstacles

This last point leads on to an exploration of the term 'growth mindset', which, along with the concept of a 'fixed mindset', was coined by Dweck (2017) in her book *Mindset: Changing the Way You Think to Fulfil Your Potential.* In the book Dweck advocates focusing on processes rather than outcomes, so that students are encouraged to place weight on developing strategies to succeed rather than being results-led.

Pupils from a very young age are highly in tune with their 'position' in the class. At primary level, they are aware of the 'hierarchy' of the table that they sit at, and pupils at senior school (and their parents) are usually keen to know how their test marks compare with those of their peers. Dweck's idea of a 'growth mindset' encourages a move away from this comparison of success. For teachers this means helping to reframe the way students measure themselves, guiding them away from rankings and league tables towards a measure of their success being the development of internal motivation, which is driven by the quest for strategies and process rather than results. Therefore, by valuing effort and procedures instead of outcomes, the focus of perceived success within the classroom will begin to shift.

EF skills help to play an important role in the development of a classroom culture that is focused on having a growth mindset, because through developing an EF-rich classroom culture, pupils will constantly be encouraged to self-evaluate and improve certain skills, which, in turn, should help to move them away from a fixed results-led mindset. For example, modelling and supporting the EF skill of setting and pursuing goals will help pupils to develop grit, perseverance and a purposeful approach. By providing meaningful praise about how pupils have applied themselves, how long they have worked at a task, how they found ways around problems or how they collaborated, you will place emphasis and praise on *the process* rather than the goal itself.

Chapter 15 on metacognition explores in more detail the skill of self-reflection and how to help pupils to take a bird's eye view of themselves to form balanced conclusions about how they are doing. By encouraging students to explicitly reflect on what worked and what did not, you will be promoting a growth mindset, and pupils will hopefully begin to identify and understand what makes them successful learners.

If you are also able to involve parents in understanding the benefits of this attitudinal change (see Chapter 16), then the student will get a clear and consistent message about what is important in their learning. Small steps that can involve parents in this shift of mindset can include incorporating explicit 'growth mindset' values rather than outcome feedback in your marking scheme, so that both pupil and parent can see what you value. This can also be incorporated into report writing and providing feedback to parents at parents' evenings. In addition, Chapter 16 consists of a series of parent guides that you could send out to parents to complement each EF skill you practise in class, so that home and school can share the same focus.

Mindfulness

An aspect of developing a growth mindset in your class might include an awareness and understanding that everyone at some point is likely to experience some anxiety, stress or distress, and for most, this is a temporary phase. Developing an open mindset to the concept that 'This, too, will pass' can empower pupils to engage in positive steps to help to foster this approach.

Teaching pupils strategies for breathing techniques to help promote mindfulness could prove a useful tool. Some teachers may want to factor it into their regular classroom practice; for others, knowing how to encourage these self-help strategies on an individual basis may be enough. There are plenty of great books on mindfulness if this is something you wish to develop to complement EF skills.

Some simple mindfulness techniques include the following:

- Encourage pupils to focus on the here and now, by concentrating on their breathing techniques.

- Students simply focus on their breathing without changing or altering it; in so doing they shift their focus on to the process of taking a breath in and out, which can reframe and redirect their attention and reduce anxiety or stress.

- Encourage students to breathe in slowly for a count of five and to release slowly for another count of five, trying to breathe from deep in the belly, or visualising trying to fill a paper bag with air as they breathe.

Building relationships of trust in the classroom

The key to working with pupils is to build a relationship of trust so that they can begin to recognise and name their challenges and seek to improve them; if you, as a teacher, are prepared to share your EF challenges (and model your strengths) with them, too, you will help enormously in breaking down some barriers and in creating a trusting environment within the class. Younger children are less inhibited and may be more willing to do this, but teenagers typically place a lot of trust in their peers, and they begin to pull away from the influence of adults, including their teachers, thus developing a trusting relationship with them is particularly important at this age.

We also need to remember that it is human nature to feel the impact of criticism more keenly than praise, and to hold on to those negative feelings longer than we bask in the glory of success. We therefore need to be mindful of this in our interactions with pupils, so as not to alienate them – even if it means drawing a line under the previous day and turning over a new leaf every day with some students.

Often, we do not even intend to impart criticism, or we are too busy and we do not realise our actions can be interpreted as not having the time for a student. More often than not our comments and actions are delivered with the best of intentions; however, how they are received and interpreted may tell a different story. We also need to be mindful of the fact that our educational system is geared towards constant judgement, one obvious example being the pass and fail of the exam system. Therefore, some students may have a lower threshold than others about how they interpret our words and actions if their self-esteem is regularly dented by the system that they are in. Discovering the strengths of the students in our classes – whether they be academic or otherwise – can help them (and us) to reframe their perceptions of themselves and become more open-minded and positive in their approach about things they find more challenging. If we can change their mood and attitude to school and learning, even those more challenging pupils may become easier to form positive relationships with.

Reframing students' self-perception

One of the ways to reframe students' self-perception and self-esteem is to help them to recognise their needs and then to assist with their self-advocacy skills. If this can become an open discussion within the classroom environment, the hope is that others would hear their classmates' strengths and challenges, and thereby become more tolerant and understanding of their peers.

Young children are very good at expressing their needs and wants, but this becomes more internalised as they grow older, and they develop an increasing awareness of social norms and a desire to 'fit in'. This can limit a pupil's willingness to be open-minded and to risk-take in the safety of a classroom environment. Teachers need to try to break down these barriers, and one of the best ways to do this is through developing an ethos of inclusion and support, as explored in this chapter.

Pupils need to learn to balance an adherence to the rules and expectations that make a school environment a workable place alongside the need to develop a growth mindset and to improve their self-awareness and education-based self-advocacy skills. Small steps can be taken by encouraging pupils to ask for help when they need it without fear of criticism or humiliation – from you or their peers. This means that teachers need to provide meaningful praise and take time to pause and consider their responses carefully to more challenging situations that they might be confronted with within a classroom environment – because pupils will gauge how open they are to safe risk-taking from their teacher's reactions to scenarios. An ethos should be fostered where pupils learn to question rather than be dependent on answers.

The classroom environment should be one where self-awareness and self-advocacy (as well as self-regulation) is accepted, and where students can understand who they are and how they learn. Once this begins to become established within the classroom, students are more likely to be proactive and take the initiative in their learning. If we encourage students to learn from their mistakes, they are more likely to avoid repeating them, which will help them to develop feelings of self-worth and self-esteem. If this is successful, they are more likely to feel like confident learners who are prepared to take risks – so how we respond is critical.

How do we know which EF skills are weaker in some students?

Your observations of the pupils you teach will provide an invaluable insight, as will discussions with parents and other teachers about their observations. Try to use these links to create the best picture you can of the students in your classroom.

If we reflect on our own childhoods and adolescence (and indeed, our adulthood) we can probably acknowledge that our EF skillset might have sometimes let us down or caused unwanted challenges. We can use our own personal experiences in these areas to help with our interactions with the children and young people we teach. It will help us to deal with them with understanding and to be considerate when scaffolding them while they develop autonomy and are ready for the support structures to be removed.

Here are some ideas to get you started:

- Reset your mindset each day and after each lesson so that you always start with a positive mindset – remember that communication is conveyed only partially by verbal communication and students will be watching and interpreting every move! A positive mindset will help to create an environment where students feel comfortable to make mistakes and learn from them.

- Allow students time to write down tasks and homework.

- Take time to quickly check planners as they record homework.

- Help to support students' working memory, and their ability to sustain their attention by repeating instructions, and if possible, backing those up in writing.

- Provide meaningful feedback.

- Pause for 3 seconds between asking a question and seeking an answer.

- Provide time checks.

- Try to build in lesson preview time so that you let students know what to expect.

- At the end of the lesson build in teacher review – where you review and recap what you have covered and what pupils have learned.

- Where possible, build in self-reflection time at the end of the lesson.

- Think about how you might set up the transition between activities – timers can help to indicate when one activity will end and another will begin.

- Develop classroom routines from the moment students enter the classroom to when they leave. These will require repetition before they become embedded as routines, and some pupils will take to them more easily than others.

- Consider what you put on the classroom walls and whether you devote an area of the wall to display the different EF skills, so that pupils are constantly exposed to them and they become part of their daily routine.

- When setting tests, get students to note the test date in their planners, but also get them to put reminders in, building up to the test.

- In the build-up to tests be clear with the students what they will be being tested and, if possible, provide summary sheets.

- Before taking tests get the students to complete a pre-test self-reflection sheet, and then afterwards a post-test reflection sheet. Factor in time for them to compare how well they thought they had prepared and whether that preparation was reflected in how they performed – and if not, to consider why.

- Consider room layout – whether to pair students with weaker EF skills with those who have EF strengths for certain tasks, to support and model.

- For younger learners have systems for cloakroom organisation – wellington boots, PE kit, coats – organised in an orderly way.

A wider school-based approach could include:

- Holding EF assemblies.

- Before school exercise / physical activity session. Diamond and Lee (2011) advocate aerobic exercise and physical activity for improving EF skills. They argue that 'Aerobic exercise robustly improves prefrontal cortex function and EFs' (Diamond and Lee 2011). Even though they are referring to this in relation to adult-based studies, exercise can help children to get ready for learning. Indeed some (in particular primary) schools have adopted routines of approximately 15 minutes of exercise at the beginning of each school day, because they observe that children respond so well to it, and it helps them to become engaged and ready to learn.

- Understanding and supporting any EF challenges colleagues have.
- A whole-school approach to EF skills in classrooms and around the school, with EF language displayed on classroom walls.

Resources

The following checklist and worksheet are for teachers to complete.

CREATING AN EF-FRIENDLY CLASSROOM CHECKLIST

Points to consider	Yes	No	'To do' list
Is your classroom an EF-friendly space?			E.g., 1. Create EF wall display 2. Provide more organisational tools / storage 3. Consider layout to place distractible students away from areas of distraction – doors, windows etc. Your own ideas: ....
Are your classroom routines effective?			E.g., 1. Routine before entering class – lining up outside? 2. Warm-up tasks set up for students at the beginning of every session 3. Learning objectives, instructions routinely written on interactive whiteboard Your own ideas: ....

Points to consider	Yes	No	'To do' list
Do you plan tasks with students' EF skills in mind?			E.g., 1. Are you clear about the task requirements? (Written down for those who need it, offering preview and review opportunities etc.) 2. Are you clear about time frame expectations (in class and for homework activities)? 3. Do you provide constructive feedback and meaningful praise with EF skills in mind? Your own ideas: ....

Do you currently model EF skills through your own actions and behaviours in class?			E.g.,
			1. Do you have good skills in all 11 EF skills?
			2. Do you model those skills by:
			  – Being punctual?
			  – Adapting well to change?
			  – Being calm and supportive?
			  – Following through on tasks and commitments?
			  – Managing time within class well?
			  – Remembering things accurately?
			  – Transitioning between activities well?
			  – Providing well thought-out and considered responses in class?
			  – Thinking before you speak?
			  – Being organised?
			  – Engaging in active listening?
			  – Being empathetic?
			  – Being aware of your own strengths and challenges?
			Your own ideas:
			....
			....
			....
			....

Do you create a positive mindset in class?			E.g., do you: 1. Have a growth mindset yourself? 2. Encourage pupils to take a risk and join in? 3. Avoid making 'quips' at pupils who have forgotten something / arrived late / blurt out etc., but deal with the situation constructively? 4. Encourage pupils to learn from their mistakes? 5. Offer support and empathy? 6. Reward process rather than results? Your own ideas: ....
Do you make learning as accessible as possible?			E.g., 1. Does the student always understand what you are asking them to do? 2. Is it always made as meaningful as possible for them – linking it to prior learning, or some other meaningful hook? 3. Do you always make it as accessible as possible for them, by being explicit about your expectations and modelling how to chunk it down to make it manageable? 4. Do you provide structured, non-critical guidance during independent learning? Your own ideas: ....

Complete this worksheet with individual students.

WORKSHEET: GETTING TO KNOW YOUR STUDENTS

About me

Favourite school subject:

. . . .

Least favourite school subject:

. . . .

Favourite teaching style:

. . . .

Least favourite teaching style:

. . . .

Best activity / time in school:

. . . .

Favourite space in school:

. . . .

What causes me to get stressed in school:

. . . .

What helps me to relax is:

. . . .

In my spare time I:

. . . .

My strengths are:

. . . .

I have difficulties with:

. . . .

I think I learn best by:

. . . .

I like it best when the teacher gets us to work...(alone, in pairs, in groups etc.):

. . . .

This worksheet is for pupils to fill in.

WORSHEET: SELF-IMPROVEMENT

Things that I would like to improve

- ☐ Being able to manage my emotions better so I do not get so upset / stressed by work / situations
- ☐ Being able to manage my time better – not waiting until the last minute
- ☐ Being able to overcome distractions to get on with / finish tasks
- ☐ Being able to hold information in my memory more effectively
- ☐ Being able to see the bigger picture / knowing what kind of learner I am
- ☐ Being able to be more organised – with my belongings or the way I tackle my work
- ☐ Being able to handle a change of plans more easily
- ☐ Being able to get started with work in a timely way

This worksheet is for teachers to fill out for each pupil.

WORKSHEET: HOW CAN I HELP YOU?

What would you like me to know about you?

. . . .

What would a good school year look like for you?

. . . .

What are the best ways I can support you to achieve this?

. . . .

EF SKILLS CHECKLIST

EF skill	Examples	Yes	No
Response inhibition	I have difficulty thinking before acting		
	I do not think about the consequences of my actions		
	I blurt things out		
Emotional control	I can get easily frustrated		
	I can get stressed		
	I can get easily upset		
	I argue back with my teacher / my peers		
	I find it hard to control my exuberance in class / with my peers		
Flexibility	I find it hard to 'go with the flow'		
	I find it hard when plans change		
	I get upset if things don't go according to plan		
	I have difficulty switching easily between tasks / moving between lesson topics		

Task initiation	I find it hard to stop doing something that interests me in order to prioritise work		
	I find it hard to get straight on with tasks		
Sustained attention	I have difficulty following through and being able to complete tasks without supervision or external pressure to complete them		
	I often start something and do not finish it		
	I find it hard to work in class for the required period without distraction		
Goal-directed persistence	I have difficulty with sticking at something		
	I start lots of things but do not complete them		
	I find it hard to complete a project		
Planning and prioritisation	I have difficulty knowing how or where to start on a task		
	I have difficulty knowing the important steps or aspects of a task		
	I have difficulty planning an essay		
Organisation	I have a messy, chaotic schoolbag		
	I have disorganised notes		
	I have difficulty finding things		
Time management	I am often late for things		
	I often find it hard to hand things in on time		
	I have difficulty maintaining routines and deadlines		
	I am not very good at knowing how long something will take		
	I miss dates and deadlines		
Working memory	I have difficulty keeping track of possessions		
	I have difficulty remembering what I am doing		
	I do not learn from past experiences		
	I have difficulty following instructions		
	I find it hard to hold maths problems / essay structures etc. in mind to successfully complete them		

EF skill	Examples	Yes	No
Metacognition	I am not sure how I learn		
	I have difficulty planning and evaluating		
	I have difficulty understanding how others see me		

CHAPTER 4

Neurodiversity, Developmental Differences and Executive Function Skills

While the previous chapters have stressed that we all have EF strengths and challenges, this chapter will specifically examine neurodiversity and associated EF challenges.

Research has shown that students with specific learning differences are more likely to show lower performance in areas of EF (Locascio *et al.* 2010) than their neurotypical peers. EF skills allow students to self-direct and self-regulate their learning and behaviour (Zelazo, Blair and Willoughby 2016), and because of the additional needs that the pupil must manage, there is more pull on the EF skills needed to help them navigate and manage their challenges.

A typical example to illustrate this could be by examining the EF skill of *planning and prioritisation* that tends to be more difficult for some neurodivergent students. A child with attention deficit hyperactivity disorder (ADHD) who is impulsive could find this particularly tricky because forward thinking and planning can be challenging for someone who is distractible. A child with a specific learning difference (SpLD), who perhaps has a weak working memory, may also find it difficult, but for a different reason, because they find it more difficult to hold information in mind and manipulate it. In this scenario they may need to keep reviewing and revisiting any task requirements, potentially causing them to work more slowly and less efficiently than some of their peers. Nonetheless, both could exhibit the same EF challenge.

Understanding the strengths and challenges in EF skills for students who have specific learning disabilities is particularly important (Zelazo *et al.* 2016) because there is an increasing amount of research to show how different specific needs are impacted by EF. A government publication in 2023 noted: 'The number of pupils with special educational needs (SEN) increased to 1.57 million pupils in 2023, representing 17.3% of all pupils' (Department for Education 2023). This means that nearly one fifth of the pupils in a classroom may have additional needs of some description. Added to which, overlapping conditions are now considered to be the norm rather than the exception, with one study suggesting that as many as 33 per cent of children who have diagnosed SEND (special educational needs and disabilities) have co-occurring difficulties with at least one learning difference, or emotional or behavioural condition. If these students can be taught how to develop their EF skills, both inside and outside the classroom, certain burdens on them will be reduced and they will be better enabled to achieve at a level commensurate with their ability (Naglieri 2005).

Attention deficit hyperactivity disorder

ADHD is often the most common neurodiverse need to be linked to EF challenges, because these pupils often struggle to regulate their emotions, avoid distraction, self-monitor, plan and prioritise, and set and pursue long-term goals.

ADHD is characterised by three different traits: inattentiveness, hyperactivity and impulsivity. It is important to remember that these characteristics can change in an individual as they develop and mature. All forms of attention deficit, including attention deficit disorder (ADD), now fall under the umbrella term of ADHD, and are categorised into one of three presentations:

- Inattentive presentation. Inattentive ADHD is characterised by failure to pay close attention to details and a tendency to make careless mistakes – the pupil may be easily distracted and often forgetful in daily activities. They may have challenges with organisation and frequently lose things, as well as having difficulties with time management. Their difficulty in sustaining attention can affect their ability to listen effectively – they may avoid tasks or dislike attempting tasks that require sustained attention and effort.

While this reads like a list of EF difficulties, these children can sometimes be overlooked in school and not flagged as falling under the ADHD umbrella because they do not possess the hyperactive trait people often associate with ADHD.

- Hyperactive-impulsive presentation. Pupils with hyperactive-impulsive presentation are often observed to fidget with their hands or feet – they may leave their seat and move around the classroom. Depending on their age, youngsters may be very active, or older learners may experience feelings of restlessness or an internal desire to move, which they try to manage, but which distracts them from focusing on the task in hand. These pupils can sometimes have difficulty engaging in activities quietly and are observed to be often on the 'go'. They may also blurt out answers and have difficulty taking turns, interrupting and intruding on others' conversations.

- Combined presentation. This is a combination of characteristics from the inattentive *and* hyperactive-impulsive presentations already described.

EF weaknesses are now understood to be core in ADHD, with individuals often having a two-to-four-year EF delay compared to their peers.

Autistic spectrum condition

Autistic children usually experience a triad of impairments focused on social communication, social interaction and social imagination (often presenting as fixed or rigid thinking). Heightened sensory processing can also be a feature. Some autistic pupils can appear socially awkward and have difficulty in understanding and managing their emotions. Because of social interaction difficulties, pupils can experience problems making and keeping friendships.

An autistic child who experiences sensory overload may present outwardly as being inattentive and more absorbed in their own internal thoughts; they may also have problems turn taking because of difficulty reading social norms. For some, there can be difficulty overriding or inhibiting impulse control to engage in an activity that holds a special interest for them; there can be inflexibility, rigid thinking, and a tendency to be routine-led. This can also inevitably impact metacognitive skills and the ability to take a bird's eye view of themselves and being able to consider how others see them.

Some common problems with EF skills can include difficulty self-monitoring, difficulties with being able to initiate a task and emotional regulation, and challenges with transitions and changes in routines as well as organisation and planning.

As with ADHD, however, sometimes pupils with an autistic spectrum condition (ASC) can go undetected in school, because many (particularly girls) have a strong desire to mask their differences so that they can 'fit in'.

Oppositional defiance disorder

This condition involves the child being defiant, negative or hostile, and as a teacher you may experience it as a sense of 'kick-back' against authority. The child can become easily irritated and defensive of themselves, and can appear to act in a deliberately obstructive way. You may experience a failure to plan and prioritise and follow instructions, because a child with an oppositional defiance disorder (ODD) wants to do things their way. There may also be task avoidance, outbursts and interruptions due to a heightened argumentativeness and a refusal to comply with adult requests. These children may display goal persisted motivation for something that they want to do, with an underlying defiance and lack of awareness of other tasks that should be being prioritised.

Specific learning differences

An SpLD is a difference or difficulty with a specific and particular aspect of learning. Common SpLDs include:

- Dyslexia, a specific difficulty primarily affecting the skills of reading, writing and spelling.

- Dyspraxia / developmental coordination disorder (DCD), difficulties primarily affecting physical coordination.

- Dyscalculia, difficulty with mathematics, primarily arithmetic, and an understanding of number sense.

- Dysgraphia, difficulty with written expression, primarily with writing.

Pupils with an SpLD can experience trouble processing and organising thoughts, sequencing difficulties, forgetfulness and working memory vulnerabilities. They may also have difficulty writing or conveying themselves on the page for a number of reasons, such as: the mechanics of writing is difficult for them, their spelling and grammar present a challenge (or number sense for mathematics), they find it hard to write neatly, or proofreading is challenging because they find it hard to spot their mistakes. This can make it harder for children to use EF skills to plan, sequence and execute tasks. A child with an SpLD may also get tired easily because of the demand that trying to manage their SpLD places on them – this may appear to manifest itself as inattention because they may appear to zone out or lose their focus if they become over-tired by the demands of the day. Due to the additional effort that they need to invest into their studies, there is also the potential for emotional dysregulation.

Conduct disorder

This is a behavioural condition where a child displays challenging anti-social, bullying and aggressive behaviour. They can display poor inhibitory control and be given to making poor decisions, wilfully or defiantly. They may also try to mount a defence and become deceitful about their actions. It may be difficult to sustain their attention because of their focus on defiance. A child with conduct disorder (CD) can also find cognitive switching hard, that is, the process of intentionally switching attention from one task to another, particularly switching from an intentionally aggravating activity to another less emotive one. Many of the EF skills will be impacted for someone with CD; for example, being able to plan and prioritise school-based activities and manage their emotions and demonstrate self-awareness and self-reflection will be affected.

Mood disorders, including bipolar disorder

EF skills can be impaired by mood disorders. Children with mood disorders may experience feelings of anxiety, low mood, lack of focus, poor sleep, poor decision making, weak working memory and disorganised thoughts. They can appear to lack motivation for tasks and show signs of inattention and poor concentration. Often mood disorders are accompanied by low self-esteem and poor emotional control and disorganised thinking.

Bipolar disorder falls under the umbrella term of mood disorder, and is characterised by mood swings – high, euphoric periods (mania) and low periods of depression. The mania stage can sometimes be misinterpreted as hyperactivity, and low states can sometimes be misinterpreted as inattention and lack of motivation. Studies have shown that bipolar disorder can impair the ability for cognitive flexibility, task completion and response inhibition.

Anxiety and depression lower mood, which will inevitably also impair efficient EF.

PART 2

SPECIFIC EXECUTIVE FUNCTION SKILLS

Each individual EF skill is explored in dedicated chapters within this part.

CHAPTER 5

Response Inhibition

EF skill	Explanation	Classroom impact
Response inhibition	Self-restraint, the capacity to think before you act, the ability to resist the urge to say or do something, allowing you time to evaluate the situation and how your behaviour may have an impact	• Acting before you think • Not thinking about the consequences • Blurting out answers / thoughts and not being able to wait until asked

What is response inhibition?

Response inhibition is the ability to think before acting and to resist being impulsive. It is the capacity to stop, change or inhibit a response that has already begun, and to ignore distractions.

Response inhibition is one of the first EF skills to develop, and it is thought by some EF specialists to be one of the most important EF skills to try to scaffold and master. The reasoning behind this is that if an individual is impulsive, they will find it hard to control their reactions, responses and attention because they lack the self-help strategies needed to regulate their behaviours and emotions. This makes it particularly hard for them to have mastery of their other EF skills. Conversely, those with good response inhibition will be able to self-regulate effectively and inhibit impulses and behaviours that are considered undesirable (e.g., in a school setting). They will also probably have developed good EF skills in other areas or be more equipped to acquire those skills, as well as potentially being more receptive to learning experiences.

Response inhibition through the ages and stages of development

- Very young children tend to be impulsive and react in the moment. Nursery age children begin to develop the skill of sharing, and they also begin to develop the ability to wait for something when asked (clips on the Marshmallow Test on YouTube show this very effectively[1]). This age group also has an increasing sense of risk and danger.

- Children aged approximately 4–7 would be expected to be able to follow classroom instructions and work on simple tasks with growing independence; they also develop a greater sense of delayed gratification and can wait for longer periods before being rewarded. They begin to learn by example and through trying things out; therefore they begin to learn to inhibit their behaviour from observation of others and from the reactions they receive.

- Children aged approximately 7–11 are more able to regulate their emotions, with a developing ability to understand personal space when interacting with their peers. They also have a better ability to work independently, and for longer periods of time.

- Those aged 11–14 will have a good understanding of the consequences of their words and behaviour on others and be better able to resist physical confrontation and provocation. They will also be developing their ability to prioritise tasks in terms of their importance.

- In the adolescent phase of development for teenagers (aged approximately 13–16) there tends to be greater external demand on them, both academically and from their peers, to conform to societal norms. This coincides with a time when they are also less prepared to accept guidance and direction from parents and family in relation to their decision making. This can therefore be a very tricky time for those who are challenged by an underdeveloped ability to inhibit their responses, meaning the teenage

---

1   See, for example, www.youtube.com/watch?v=2xMgHKxukro

years can be more turbulent for them and they are more prone to social exclusion. Therefore, the ability to gain mastery over this EF skill for this age group will make an enormous difference to how they function in school, and in their life more generally.

What you might see in a pupil with poor inhibitory control

- They need to go first.

- They blurt things out (they do not wait their turn).

- They push to the front of a line (e.g., in the lunch queue).

- When told to get equipment out, they grab things without thinking about others.

- They react in the heat of the moment.

- They do not listen to all of the instructions before getting started.

It is important to remember that impulsive actions tend not to be backed up with thought, so the skill we are trying to improve with this EF is to encourage pupils to pause, stop and think before they respond to a trigger; this is particularly relevant to pupils with ADHD.

Inhibitory control in the classroom

Initially we need to raise pupils' awareness of what good response inhibition looks like, which we can do through class-based activities. We can also model strategies and verbalise inhibitory control and thought processing ourselves, so that pupils become more aware of it, and it becomes accepted language within the classroom. So, for example, when a pupil shows good self-control by putting their hand up to answer a question rather than blurting it out, this is praised and acknowledged, so that those who find it more challenging witness positive reinforcement of good inhibitory control in practice. Once there is an understanding of what this EF skill is, pupils can then be encouraged to work on their own ability to inhibit their responses.

Teachers can help pupils to develop their response inhibition by encouraging them to consider what their own inhibitory goals are, that is, the areas that they themselves – perhaps with the teacher's discreet direction – identify as areas of personal weakness in terms of their classroom behaviour. One way of doing this is to get pupils to work together to brainstorm possible triggers and then to develop an accepted routine for them to work through to address the issue. For example, a set of common classroom inhibitory control difficulties could be identified with suggested solutions for pupils to follow. While this can be chatted through, a visual reminder will probably have a more lasting impact and will be something individual pupils can refer back to, whereas they may struggle to recall a conversation or verbal instruction.

The following checklist will help teachers gauge how well they support response inhibition in the classroom.

TEACHER SELF-REVIEW CHECKLIST: RESPONSE INHIBITION

I support students' response inhibition by:	Yes	No
Being calm and in control		
Having a clear set of classroom expectations that I am consistent with, and which are displayed visually around the classroom		
Not interrupting when pupils are talking to me; I let them finish their sentence		
Trying to remind myself that when a child loses control of their response inhibition that they are not intentionally being 'naughty', and I react fairly and with understanding		
Counting to three before I expect a pupil to answer a question – meaning I give those who need it longer to think, and those who want to blurt the answer out the expectation that they need to control their impulse by counting to three in their heads		
Having a classroom with minimal distractions		
Being aware of those pupils with response inhibition challenges; I give them preferential seating – at the front / back of the class		
Providing opportunities for 'brain breaks' in class to allow pupils to stretch and refocus		

Ways you can model and support students to develop their own response inhibition

- Keep a clutter-free environment, with minimal distractions.

- Provide written instructions (on the whiteboard / laptops / printed out) to back up verbal instructions, so that the pupils can tick off the steps / instructions as they complete them.

- Consider the seating plan in your classroom, giving preferential seating to those who need it – away from distractions / sitting with a good role model / position in class (front or back). If there is no set seating plan, encourage pupils to make sensible seating choices.

- Create systems for responding to pupils. Tell them you will count to three / five / whatever number you choose before you take any answers – this gives time for pupils to think, but also helps inhibit those who blurt out, because they can hear you counting. This could become silent counting once the routine is embedded. For those who constantly interrupt or have many things they want to contribute, ask them to write down what they want to say on Post-it® notes and let them know you will make time to talk to them before the lesson ends. If they know you will do this, it will help to teach them to hold on to their thoughts or questions because they know you will make time for them.

- If a pupil is emotionally dysregulated – upset / feels an injustice / is very excited etc. – build in a consistent routine where they need to take three deep breaths before talking.

Classroom ideas for teachers to help with response inhibition

How you support pupils' response inhibition will depend on the age of the child(ren) involved. Here are some suggestions:

- Develop and extend the time that a pupil is able to wait to do a desirable task or to be rewarded (known as delayed gratification), thereby also helping their ability to prioritise less appealing but higher priority tasks. Delayed gratification can be explored within a classroom setting by, for example, encouraging pupils to work towards a delayed positive goal – a class reward system where each pupil works towards a common class goal of a 'treat' once a certain number of rewards have been earned.

- Develop an understanding of cause and effect and consequences of actions – e.g., working with students to practise restraint regarding chatting in class / internet usage / completing set tasks first.

- Work with pupils to extend their thoughts to long-term goals rather than reacting in the here and now.

- Work with pupils to develop their skills to look at themselves from the outside in – what would they be recommending to themselves that they do in this situation (metacognition)?

- Help pupils develop the ability to break down tasks and work into more accessible and manageable pieces, so that it feels easier to tackle.

- Work with pupils to employ metacognitive skills for self-talk so that they can talk themselves down from escalating thoughts or emotions and inhibit their immediate responses. You will need to regularly model and show pupils to learn how to 'self-talk', so that when a situation arises, they can pause and say to themselves 'good choice / bad choice'. They will need to practise how to stop and think, and you will need to encourage them to reflect afterwards, so that they can begin to learn from their mistakes. It is important to discuss plausible solutions with the pupil(s). By doing this you are helping them to think about the things that might be causing them some difficulty, but without it being in the heat of the moment – therefore their more 'rational' brain should be able to come up with some good solutions – e.g., 'I can help control my response of getting anxious by asking my teacher to...'

- If there are opportunities at the end of tasks, or while you are waiting for everyone to arrive, build in games like Simon Says, 20 Questions, Red Light Green Light or I Spy, and make sure you have established rules about how pupils respond.

As you work through the rest of the chapters in this book that focus on each of the remaining different EF skills, you will notice that this list very much overlaps with, and involves, some of the other EF skills – as high-lighted at the beginning of this chapter, the EF of response inhibition is very important, and involves many crossovers with the other EF skills.

Resources

The following worksheet is for pupils to create and complete with teacher guidance; it can be adapted depending on the ages of the children involved and its suitability.

WORKSHEET: RESPONSE INHIBITION PROBLEM SOLVING

Depending on the age of the child, this worksheet will have more impact if the pupil creates their own version. You could use this as a data-gathering exercise by using a self-rating style questionnaire to gauge pupils' percep-tions of themselves. By recording the solutions in chart form, the pupil can refer to them when the rational side of their brain has been overtaken by impulsivity.

You might take pupils through the following steps:

1. Discuss, identify and make a note of any areas where the pupil strug-gles to control their responses – e.g., getting angry quickly, becoming anxious in certain situations, blurting things out, interrupting con-versations, or whatever other 'response inhibition' the pupil experi-ences, such as the ability to control exuberant reactions, or getting overwhelmed by anger or sadness or even hilarity.

2. Ask the pupil to choose the solutions that they prefer.

3. Talk about what will happen if the first solution doesn't work.

4. Make a visual reminder.

It will be important to acknowledge with the pupil that they will not develop immediate mastery of this skill, but they should keep practising. They should learn to congratulate themselves when they do exert some impulse control – this will also probably need to be modelled by you, until they get into the habit themselves of practising positive 'self-talk'.

A pupil's self-made worksheet could look something like this, personalised to include the points that you have brainstormed when discussing the build-up to this activity.

Activity	Strong skillset	Room for improvement	Weak skillset
I can avoid distractions			
I can hold on to my thoughts and don't blurt them out			
I am good at monitoring my phone usage			
I am good at monitoring my internet usage			
I can stop gaming when I need to			
Other ideas...			

FOR THOSE PUPILS WHO NEED ADDITIONAL, MORE FOCUSED SUPPORT WITHIN THE CLASSROOM

1. Set clear rules and expectations. Try to provide explicit, and clear, rules, which are regularly reinforced – if they can be displayed visually in the classroom, even better! This will help those children who need more support in this area to understand when and how they have overstepped the boundary. Praise and / or rewards can help with reinforcing these expectations and tend to work better than negative responses and sanctions. Disinhibited children often require more frequent check-ins from the teacher.

2. Limit distractions. Consider the visual and auditory distractions surrounding the child – this will include other children, activities or even classroom displays that can pull their attention away from a task.

3. Strategic seating. Consider careful placement in the classroom. Seating them near you can allow you to discreetly re-engage them, make regular eye contact and enable them to feel more involved; however, this may not always be the best place for them. They may work well with another member of the class, or in a small group with good peer role models. Alternatively, they may be better being seated at the back so that they do not disturb other students as easily – this strategic placement may also give them the opportunity to stand (and therefore fulfil a possible desire to wriggle and move) to complete some of their work, if this is an acceptable compromise for you and the way you run and manage your class.

INTERVENTIONS

1. Teach response delay. Encourage strategies such as counting to five or ten before responding verbally or physically.

2. Verbalise plans. If the pupil is very hasty to get started on work and does not plan, consider asking them to verbalise a plan of approach before getting started to allow for better planning and a more strategic approach.

3. Take periodic breaks. Allowing very short breaks of just 1 or 2 minutes may help the child to reset and refocus – a short break to fill a water bottle, take a bathroom break or bring their work to you for review provides opportunities for them to leave their seat and move. These breaks do need to be well managed and time-limited, so if the child goes to the bathroom or fills a water bottle, the expectation must be that they are back in class within a finite set period of time.

4. Set goals for accuracy. If the child has a desire to rush through their work, acknowledge the fact that they have completed their work to help them feel good about their accomplishments, but then set additional goals such as reviewing their work for accuracy or neatness etc.

5. Provide positive reinforcement. Positive consequence-based systems may be effective. Positive reinforcement for appropriate behaviours will probably work more effectively than negative consequences, which may not decrease problem behaviours.

■ CHAPTER 6 ■

Emotional Control

EF skill	Explanation	Classroom impact
Emotional control	The ability to regulate your emotions The ability to conduct healthy personal and school-based relationships	• Getting easily frustrated • Getting stressed • Getting easily upset • Arguing back with teacher / pupils • Finding it hard to control exuberance in class / with peers

What is emotional control?

Just as with response inhibition, emotional control is one of the key EF skills that will help to determine an individual's success with their other EF skills. Response inhibition and emotional control are, to a certain extent, co-dependent: you must be emotionally regulated in order to control responses, and you have to be able to control your responses in order to be emotionally regulated. Without good emotional control it is hard to plan or organise, sustain working memory or self-reflect, to name just some of the other EF skills.

What you might see in a pupil who struggles with emotional control

• They have a tendency to react quickly or spontaneously.

• They have difficulty receiving negative feedback.

- They show an emotional response that is stronger than their peers exhibit, or that is greater than expected.

- They find it difficult to maintain perspective and see the bigger picture.

- They find it hard to see the other person's perspective.

- They find it hard to move on and forget about it.

For pupils with a particular vulnerability in this area, strong emotional reactions can come and go quite quickly.

In order to help pupils to understand their emotional responses to different scenarios, teachers need to have some understanding of the brain processes that control emotional responses. How much of this understanding you then convey to pupils will depend on the age of the pupils you teach.

If children have a basic understanding of the physiology of the brain, they can start to rationalise how they feel. It is helpful for them to know that the amygdala is part of the human brain that is often called the 'reptilian' brain, because it was important in centuries past, when cavemen and women needed a heightened sense of their 'fight, flight, freeze or fawn' responses in the face of danger to ensure survival. Understanding that the reptilian brain is still part of the physiology of our modern brains, and that it overrides any 'rational' response because it is 'hard-wired' for self-preservation, in whatever form that looks like when faced with the threat of a modern-day danger (being scared, angry or upset), can help children to visualise and better understand the changes that take place in the brain in the moments when they experience heightened emotional dysregulation.

Older children can take this level of understanding a little further and can be taught that when the 'reptilian' part of our brain (the amygdala) feels under pressure it releases cortisol, which is a stress hormone. In this state no learning can take place and understanding others' perspectives becomes very difficult; it can also inhibit the ability to 'think' your way out of a problem.

The more children – even quite young children – can understand about the brain, the more empowered they are to understand the range of feelings that they might experience, and the more equipped they can become at being able to name and identify their emotions. Once they are able to do this, the next step is learning to engage in self-talk to rationalise the more negative emotions they might feel before they become too triggered so that they can 'talk down' the 'reptilian' brain, before it takes over.

Ways you can model and support students to help them to regulate themselves better

- Encourage them to 'breathe through' the emotional surge.

- Practise relaxation techniques with them.

- Anticipate and visualise some of the more positive emotions they will feel when the moment of emotional dysregulation passes, which will help the moment to pass more quickly.

- Being aware of their emotional responses and how to manage them will help children to:

    - Take a step back and pause before reacting

    - Walk away from the situation so as not to inflame it further

    - Allow a cooling off time

    - See the bigger picture, as well as promoting seeing things from someone else's perspective.

Bystanders can also be taught not to react to an outburst of emotional dysregulation and to walk away from a situation that might become difficult.

Remember, also, that just because emotional outbursts are not necessarily witnessed at school, it does not mean that pupils have mastery over this EF. At home children do not have to 'hold it together' and inhibit their responses in the same way as they do in front of their peers when at school. Therefore, they may manage their behaviour and reactions less well when they are in their 'safe' environment, and family members can often feel the brunt of it with children having meltdowns and acting more rashly than they might otherwise if they were at school. It is important to 'hear' parents when they relay these facts or snippets of information about their child because it will give you a greater understanding and insight into their functioning with this EF skill.

Daniel Siegel's 'Flipping your lid' model

One visual that is often effective with children, and that can help to develop emotional intelligence, helps them to understand what happens when they experience emotional dysregulation. Daniel Siegel's hand model of the brain is very effective in demonstrating the concept of 'flipping your lid', when the 'reptilian' part of the brain takes over in times of emotional distress.[1] Even very young children can be taught to understand their emotional responses using this model. The depth and level of explanation about what it represents can be tailored to the age of the child, and it can be suitable from primary right through to sixth form pupils; the older the pupil, the greater the depth of technical explanation can be provided.

Unavoidable emotional challenges

It is also important to be aware that there are some unavoidable factors or triggers in an individual's life that may mean, for some, that their emotional control can (temporarily) become even more challenged:

- Transitioning to secondary school where there are more social and academic demands and more projects that require long-term planning can be particularly hard for some pupils. This period of time is often coupled with decreasing parental scaffolding, which has, up until this point, created a routine for the child and made life more predictable.

- An increased desire for independence can lead to an increase in emotional dysregulation because more demands are placed on the pupil, which they must try to manage on their own. Some teenagers, particularly those with ADHD, typically require ongoing support and scaffolding for longer than their neurotypical peers.

- The teenage years in general can create greater challenges for some pupils, because they are dealing with puberty and increased

---

1   The concept of 'flipping your lid' is demonstrated by Daniel Siegel in his YouTube video, www.youtube.com/watch?v=gm9CIJ74Oxw

hormone levels, which can make them more emotional. It is important to remember that girls can have a monthly exacerbation of this, when their oestrogen levels are low.

- Other challenges in a young person's life can also dysregulate their emotions for a period of time – divorce, death and house moves are just some of the key triggers to be mindful of.

The following checklist will help teachers gauge how well they support emotional control in the classroom.

TEACHER SELF-REVIEW CHECKLIST: EMOTIONAL CONTROL

I support students' emotional control by:	Yes	No
Being calm and in control and using a well-regulated voice		
Reinforcing positive behaviour		
Understanding and supporting emotional dysregulation rather than being judgmental		
Trying to remind myself that when a child loses control of their response inhibition that they are not intentionally being 'naughty' and I react fairly and with understanding		
Creating a trusting, supportive classroom environment		
Engaging in active listening		
Understanding and being supportive of mistakes, and using them to encourage pupils to learn from them		
Maintaining a neutral stance in times of conflict		

Ways you can model and support students to develop their own emotional control

- Model appropriate emotional control by talking aloud and 'walking students through' a situation that provokes feelings of anger or sadness; explain how they could deal with their feelings.

- Increase children's awareness of the impact of their behaviours and reactions on others. Discussing a recent situation with them and how they reacted and suggesting other ways they might approach a similar situation in the future will help to demonstrate how they might respond differently and thereby increase their self-awareness.

- Create a supportive listening environment and get into the routine of creating time to review and reflect on behaviours and set goals to help to overcome obstacles. This helps students to self-reflect and develop their own strategies to manage their emotions.

- Encourage and model help strategies such as 'self-talk' for times when things don't go according to plan. You could consider role-playing some scenarios to help pupils learn how to manage events. This will help pupils to build up strategies where they are more equipped to talk themselves down from a sense of emotional dysregulation. As the teacher you should also consider using out-loud self-talk, when appropriate, so pupils can hear and learn what you would like them to be able to do.

- Try to be supportive and not show any sense of disapproval about an outburst of emotional dysregulation from a student. Remember the reference to Mehrabian's analysis of communication discussed in the Introduction, which identified that only 7 per cent of what is said is used by the recipient to interpret our interaction with them, compared to 38 per cent tonality, volume and tempo and 55 per cent non-verbal signals.[2] Therefore, how you respond to the pupil is key. Try not to respond with a negative emotional reaction or jump to conclusions, because otherwise your body language may relay what you are thinking. Consider the pupil's personal space. And try to be calm.

Classroom ideas for teachers to help with emotional control

- Having clear and specific SMART classroom / school rules (specific, measurable, attainable, relevant and time-bound) that pupils know about, and that are possible to follow, helps pupils

---

2   See https://worldofwork.io/2019/07/mehrabians-7-38-55-communication-model

to be able to predict what their classroom experience will be like, and this predictability helps them to manage their emotions. For example, the expectation is always to line up outside the classroom before being invited in by the teacher; the expectation is to sit in allocated seats; the expectation is to start an independent (provided) warm-up activity, while waiting for the lesson to start.

- Routines also create predictability for students.

- Change is inevitable and interruptions to the daily school / class routine do unavoidably occur. Teachers can help students to manage this, and thereby help emotional dysregulation or anxiety caused by the changes, by giving them as much prior warning about this as possible.

- Promoting the benefit of exercise to relieve stress and tension, and promoting healthy sleeping habits, while not under the control of the teacher, will help to reinforce how emotions are connected to general well-being, and encourage students to consider these as self-help strategies and positive thinking.

- Teach response-delay techniques, similar to those used to help with response inhibition (e.g., practise leaving the situation, counting before responding, developing two or more possible responses). To promote agency and investment in the process, encourage pupils to think through the potential ramifications of their response. Consider brainstorming a series of steps / responses with the class and recording them as a visual reminder.

- You could consider getting into a routine at the beginning / end of the lesson of practising calming exercises to help them to prepare for the lesson ahead or the transition to the next lesson.

Activities that could form part of PSHE (personal, social, health and economic education) / form time / tutor time / circle time could include:

- Brainstorming 'feelings' words, both positive and negative, and then discussing them and what triggers those feelings. Brainstorm strategies to harness or to control those emotions.

- Talking about where they feel their emotions in their body.

- Visualising positive feelings and emotions. Practising this means you can then remind pupils to use their visualisation techniques if they are becoming emotionally dysregulated.

- Discussing stress – you can reinforce that certain levels of stress are good for motivation to succeed, so that pupils know that those feelings can be okay as long as they do not tip into having too much stress or an overly negative stress response to something. Brainstorm what causes stress in the school day, to help students become more aware of their stress triggers so that they understand them and can prevent them where possible, and know how to manage them if not. This can empower students if they learn that they *can* control emotions, but they need to be able to recognise them first.

- Encouraging those pupils who need it to think about who their 'safe' person in school to talk to is.

- Raising awareness of body language, both other people's and their own. This will help pupils to see when someone is beginning to experience stress, and they can then use strategies to try to calm the situation down.

- Practising calming / breathing / mindfulness strategies with students.

You can choose the strategies that might work in your classroom, with your collection of pupils, but it is important to remember that you should only do what you feel comfortable and confident doing. If necessary, for some pupils who have needs that might extend beyond your remit, you should enlist the help of others in the school more qualified to support them.

It is also important to remember that some strategies will need to be modelled and revisited regularly to help to embed them – expecting students to be able to manage their emotions better and become more self-equipped after one or two demonstrations is just not feasible.

Resources

The following two worksheets are for pupils to complete.

WORKSHEET: MANAGING YOUR EMOTIONS

1. Become aware of how you are feeling.

2. Give a name to that emotion – sadness, joy, anger, anxiety etc.

3. Identify any physical impacts of how you are feeling, how your body responds.

4. Identify what has made you feel like this.

5. Accept that this is how you feel *right now* but acknowledge that this will pass.

6. Consider if you should practise any techniques to help you deal with this emotion – breathing exercises, mindfulness, taking a walk, thinking of positive things in your life etc.

Your own ideas...

. . . .

. . . .

. . . .

. . . .

WORKSHEET: SELF-REGULATION

1. How will you notice when emotional dysregulation is affecting you?

   My thoughts:

   . . . .

   . . . .

   . . . .

2. How will you help yourself not to react too quickly?

My thoughts:

. . . .

. . . .

. . . .

3. How can you manage how you react?

My thoughts:

. . . .

. . . .

. . . .

4. If you do react, do you need to build any bridges with anyone?

My thoughts:

. . . .

. . . .

. . . .

My own ideas...

. . . .

. . . .

. . . .

. . . .

. . . .

. . . .

. . . .

FOR THOSE PUPILS WHO NEED ADDITIONAL, MORE FOCUSED SUPPORT WITHIN THE CLASSROOM

Pupils who have a heightened sense of emotional dysregulation may need an extra level of emotional support – this may be due to a specific learning need, a medical condition or because of past trauma. It is important to try to remember this, even when the pupil might be at their most challenging and dysregulated – they will need compassion and understanding.

For those pupils whose emotional dysregulation can escalate quickly, it can take a disproportionate amount of time for them to come back down to a baseline. This means that during this dysregulated state, no learning will be taking place, and therefore, for many reasons – from well-being to education – this should be avoided at all costs, by becoming more aware of those pupils in your class who might be perceived as being disruptive or emotionally reactive, and trying to anticipate and avoid trigger events.

The way to support and scaffold improvements in emotional dysregulation is by providing as supportive an environment as possible. For those pupils who need additional support, there may need to be flexibility within the school day and in the physical make-up of the school for them to have access to a neutral room, which allows them space and time to decompress. This can be a significant lifeline for them.

However, the provision of an additional space can be a luxury that many schools cannot offer, so consideration could be given, for those few individuals who might need it, to develop other strategies, such as the ability to 'walk it off', or whatever other strategies your setting can offer.

Some suggested strategies:

- Allow a cooling-off period, where the pupil is not challenged or asked to explain their outburst – this allows them time to calm down and to self-reflect.

- Consider traffic light cards for the pupil to use to indicate their state of emotional regulation, with a pre-agreed process used by the teacher to respond to them – e.g., an orange card means the pupil can be encouraged to practise calming techniques but does not need to leave the class, and a red card might indicate a sufficient level of emotional arousal that the pupil needs to 'walk it off' for a couple of minutes / seek support from the other professionals in school.

- Some pupils may require greater support than you are able to offer them within the classroom environment, and you may have to use the pastoral processes available within your school, to provide additional input for them.

CHAPTER 7

Flexibility

EF skill	Explanation	Classroom impact
Flexibility	The ability to be adaptable and to be willing to change plans and direction, where needed	• Finding it hard to 'go with the flow' • Finding it hard when plans change • Getting upset if things don't go according to plan • Difficulty switching easily between tasks / moving between lesson topics – wanting to finish a previous task and finding it hard to move on

What is flexibility?

Being able to shift flexibly between situations, activities or aspects of a problem is an essential component of self-regulation.

Flexibility is the ability to 'go with the flow' and not get thrown by last-minute changes. Someone demonstrates flexibility when they are able to adapt and revise plans when conditions change, for example when obstacles and setbacks arise, when new information becomes available, or when mistakes occur. It is the ability to manage disappointment and upset when changes arise and be able to problem solve and find other solutions. Flexibility can also be the ability to initiate or inhibit behaviours and adapt to the changing environment – in other words, having the ability to remain emotionally stable and self-regulated in order to have the mental capacity to be able to think flexibly.

Conversely, inflexibility can cause an emotional outburst when faced with change, and it is often characterised by rigid inflexible thinking patterns.

What you might see in a pupil who struggles with flexibility

- They find it hard to manage changes in the school day.

- They find it hard to tackle a task because their solution has not worked, and they are not able to look at it objectively and think of other ways around it.

- They get stuck on one solution or one way of looking at a problem and find it hard to see other solutions.

- They have trouble coming up with topics or generating ideas for things to write about.

- They have difficulty coping with open-ended homework assignments (e.g., they do not know what to write about or where to start).

- They have difficulty dealing with changes in plans or routines, such as the presence of a supply teacher or a change in timetable.

- They have difficulty coming up with a Plan B if Plan A didn't work.

- They have difficulty participating in group work.

Students need to learn to have appropriate reactions to scenarios as well as to be able to move from one activity to another, by taking things in their stride. They also need to be able to look at situations from different perspectives, to see others' points of view. However, if you have pupil(s) in the classroom who find transitions and change difficult, or who struggle to shift from one activity to another, try to be supportive and not assume they are acting up or being stubborn on purpose – understanding potential difficulties with flexibility and helping the student to put strategies in place could prevent a situation from escalating.

The following checklist will help teachers gauge how well they support flexibility in the classroom.

TEACHER SELF-REVIEW CHECKLIST: FLEXIBILITY

I support students' flexibility by:	Yes	No
Displaying classroom rules clearly		
Setting out my classroom expectations clearly at the beginning of each term		
Notifying students in advance of any changes in routine within my class, e.g.: • Letting them know I will be absent on a course etc. • Any room rearrangement – seating plans etc. • Any change in venue		
Notifying them and reminding them about tests		
Having a timeline / lesson structure on the whiteboard for them to follow		
Using timers, clocks and reminders to signal when the activity will stop / change		
Being mindful of the time needed for transition – to another class or between subject areas – and allowing sufficient time to prepare for that transition by tidying away and recording any homework etc.		
Previewing new work		
Notifying them about any changes beyond the classroom that might impact their day		
Being available for / understanding of those who need additional support to adjust to change		
Your own ideas...		

Ways you can model and support students to develop their own flexibility

- To help pupils to develop the skills and independence to deal with inflexibility on their own, without you needing to scaffold, they need to learn what flexibility is. Therefore, try to keep to schedules and stick to the plan where possible.

- Where this is not possible, handle changes by verbally rehearsing with pupils what is likely to happen so that you model the process of adapting to change using 'self-talk'. This can help them to visualise the change.

- Preview and review things by verbalising your thoughts and processes so the pupils can witness you assessing how they did and what you might do differently next time.

- Where possible, give choices, because that allows for a feeling of control.

- Have specific rules and boundaries.

- Use visuals, such as calendars; lists and schedules can also be used to plot things such as activities / actions / demands. They can also help someone to adapt and plan for changes by visually showing what event might have been subject to a change of date etc. The use of other visuals like timers and clocks reinforces the movement of time.

Classroom ideas for teachers about how to help with flexibility

- Whenever possible, provide advance notice or warning of what is coming next – if you are a form teacher, consider perhaps making time to preview the day's timetable with the class at the beginning of the day, and notify them of any changes that you know about. Encourage colleagues to notify you of any changes that it would be helpful for you to share with your class. If you are a class teacher, keeping your class updated about any changes to their timetable is also very useful.

- For changes that you know are inevitable, introduce them gradually to help the children to prepare.

- Use external guides / visuals to assist with the concept of change – consider displaying a daily schedule and reviewing it at the outset of the day and noting the known changes on it; this can help a child anticipate the sequence of events and can serve as a useful reminder of any changes in the daily routine.

- Try to maintain schedules and routines whenever possible, while building in the possibility of flexibility – if you teach secondary pupils or older, discuss with them the requirement to check their email and any school contact systems, so that they are encouraged to take responsibility for any last-minute notifications about change that they might receive. Sow the seed with them that they need to be prepared for something like this if it happens.

- In general, help pupils to anticipate what they might encounter in a situation – the more information they have in advance, the more they will feel able to cope and navigate the unexpected situation.

- Help pupils to come up with a few default strategies for handling situations where flexibility causes the most problems – this can include simple things like walking away from the situation for some cooling off time, and then returning and asking a specific person for help, employing calming strategies.

- Encourage pupils to engage in self-talk, to deal with change, and then encourage review and reflection after the event, about how they handled it and how they might learn from their responses.

- Do not assume pupils who have difficulty with flexibility will be able to generalise from one situation to another and understand what they need to do in the new situation – provide them with cues to remind them.

- Prepare for change with alerts. The 2-minute warning is an effective tool to alert pupils that one activity is about to end and another will begin. Also allowing a couple minutes of downtime activities can help with transitions.

- Setting time limits for tasks before the child begins the next task is also useful and helps with adjustment to the change in activity.

This also teaches pupils to understand the concept of time and how long tasks may take. An analogue clock (as opposed to a digital one) can also help demonstrate the concept of time by the movement of the hands.

- Using peer modelling to show good flexibility can also be helpful to model that it is time to change, cueing other pupils in by their shift in behaviour to move on to the next task.

- Raise awareness that the changes we need to adapt to can be because of both internal influences (e.g., changes in mood, stress) and external influences (e.g., changes in routine or staff).

- Encourage pupils to notice any physical warning signs of inflexibility (muscle tightness, breathing changes) and encourage them to ask themselves if this particular situation is important to them or not – and, depending on their reaction, whether they can find a way to be flexible.

- Encourage them to think about what could go wrong, and what their Plan B might be.

- Encourage them to think about whether there is another way to think about a scenario that they are finding difficult to handle.

- Devise some coping strategies together, e.g.:

  - Discuss the benefits of getting enough sleep and exercise and the positive effect of these on general emotional stability.

  - Encourage pupils to consider whether any relaxation strategies could become a regular part of their routine – such as breathing techniques, mindfulness etc. – to help to keep them emotionally regulated when they feel that they might be about to spiral.

  - Encourage pupils to engage in the thought process about whether and how to remove themselves from any stress triggers (where appropriate).

  - Encourage self-talk – e.g., 'I can do this' or 'This, too, will pass'.

Resources

The following checklist will help pupils to increase their self-awareness of what their possible triggers are.

FLEXIBILITY CHECKLIST

Flexibility difficulty	Yes / no	My comments
When I don't succeed the first time, I tend to give up / find it hard to think of a new approach		
If plans or routines change, I find it hard to adapt		
I have problems with open-ended classwork / homework assignments (e.g., I don't know what to write about / where to start)		

Here are some self-help strategies for pupils.

Tips	Self-talk
Notice the physical warning signs of inflexibility (muscle tightness, breathing changes) and ask yourself if you can find a way to be flexible	Big deal or little deal?
Whenever you have to make a decision about something, ask yourself 'What could go wrong and what's Plan B if this doesn't work?'	What are your options? What is your Plan B? Is there another way to think about this?

Other strategies:	Your own idea(s):

Here are some ideas for pupils to make their own worksheet with guidance from their teachers. Pupils should keep the worksheet to refer to in the future.

WORKSHEET: FLEXIBILITY / PROBLEM SOLVING

1. Identify the problem.

2. Brainstorm solutions.

3. Ask the pupil to choose the solution(s) that they prefer.

4. Discuss Plan A, and if that doesn't work, what is their Plan B?

5. Make a visual reminder.

6. Self-reflect: What went well? What might I do differently next time?

EXAMPLE WORKSHEET: FLEXIBILITY / PROBLEM SOLVING

1. What is the problem?

   I get panicky if I feel I do not understand something in a lesson.

2. How might I begin to solve the problem?

   Tell the teacher I've got a bit lost and wait for them to help me.

   Take deep breaths to try to calm myself down...(or whatever other strategies work for the pupil).

3. What solutions do you prefer?

   List the priorities of Plan A, B, C etc.

4. Start with Plan A.

   I know I can talk to my teacher and say I got lost and am unclear...

5. If that doesn't work, move on to Plan B.

   I know I can ask my classmate to help to explain.

6. Self-reflect: What went well? What might I do differently next time?

IDEAS FOR DEVELOPING COPING STRATEGIES IN PUPILS

- Encourage relaxation strategies becoming a regular part of their routine, such as breathing techniques, mindfulness etc., to help to keep them emotionally regulated when they feel that they might be about to spiral.

- Encourage removal from the stress trigger (where appropriate).

- Encourage self-talk, e.g., 'I can do this' or 'This, too, will pass'.

- Let them know it is okay to ask for help.

- Some pupils may benefit from writing down their thoughts – what we now might call 'journaling'.

- Creating lists of the available options (and for some, including their pros and cons) can help to create perspective and distance from the problem(s), and provide clarity about how to proceed.

- Take a time-limited break (using a timer to regulate the amount of time spent) to escape from the stress trigger. Returning to it afterwards may become easier because of the time spent away from it.

FOR THOSE PUPILS WHO NEED ADDITIONAL, MORE FOCUSED SUPPORT WITHIN THE CLASSROOM

- If you know what changes and unexpected events cause them anxiety (a missed lesson or work notification), reduce panic by breaking tasks down so they only have to complete one step at a time, and if you can make the time, walk them through the anxiety-producing situation.

- If you can talk about it and confront it and come up with some strategies to manage it, the pupil will benefit enormously from this small input in time – and you may find that in your class they are able to become more regulated, over time, because they know that you are supportive of them.

- If you cannot create the time to support this extra level of input because of teaching commitments, encourage the pupil to find a trusted adult within the school who can help them – this could be a form tutor, school counsellor or ELSA (emotional literacy support assistant), or any other adult they feel comfortable with, who can make some time to discuss strategies with the pupil. If the pupil has a trusted close friend at school, then peer support can also be very effective – if this is something facilitated by you, rather than between the pupils themselves, it will be important for you to check and to know that the friend is happy to fulfil the role of talking about the unexpected change and helping the pupil to get it back into perspective.

CHAPTER 8

Task Initiation

EF skill	Explanation	Classroom impact
Task initiation	The ability to start tasks without putting them off	• Finding it hard to stop doing something that interests you in order to prioritise work (playing online games, social media etc.) • Finding it hard to get straight on with tasks set by the teacher – requiring input to get started or using strategies (sharpening pencils, going to the loo, filling a water bottle) to put off starting

What is task initiation?

Task initiation is the ability to begin projects or activities without procrastination, in an efficient and timely manner, and being able to independently generate ideas, responses or problem-solving strategies.

Using this skill can involve beginning a task as soon as it is assigned or deciding when a task will be done and beginning it promptly at that predetermined time.

Difficulties with task initiation can be shown in a few ways:

- Academically, e.g., having trouble getting started on tasks and homework.

- Behaviourally, e.g., finding it hard to get started on physical activities.

- Cognitively, e.g., coming up with ideas or planning.

Different tasks place varying demands on initiation, and depending on the student's level of interest, in what they are doing – therefore you may see varying levels of task initiation from the same person depending on the tasks at hand.

When promoting task initiation in school the ultimate goal is to be able to move the student away from a state of enforced external pressure imposed by you, as the teacher, to meet deadlines and so forth, to a state in which internal motivation takes over and the student has a self-driven desire to succeed. However, younger children and those older ones who have not developed good task initiation skills will not have developed these skills and will still be reliant on deadlines, rewards and punishments.

Difficulties with task initiation include:

- Not knowing how to get started – feeling overwhelmed
- Believing the task will 'take forever'
- Thinking they are not up to the job and so delaying to avoid failure
- Lacking motivation to start the task
- Difficulty re-engaging with a task after taking a break
- Delaying starting something because there are better / more interesting things to do first
- Not liking the topic
- Feeling tentative about starting new tasks.

Why students might procrastinate and avoid initiating tasks

Procrastination is often linked to ADHD and a difficulty with focus distractibility; however, we all have the ability to procrastinate. If a task feels overwhelming, and / or too big to tackle, a natural reaction is to put it to the bottom of the 'to do' list or pile of jobs and to get on with smaller, more manageable activities.

Procrastination can also feature if a task feels boring and / or there is no motivation to complete it, or if there is a fear of not being able to complete it.

How difficulty with procrastination may cause a problem in school

- If a student has a tendency to procrastinate, they may miss deadlines, or realise that deadlines are rapidly approaching and will therefore produce work of a reduced quality due to lack of time.

- This can often be accompanied by a self-fulfilling sense of low self-worth because the work is not of the standard the student wanted to achieve, or a sense of anxiety and panic at failing to meet a deadline.

- If a student experiences this too often, they may go into self-protection mode and self-sabotage their ability to succeed to try to avoid feelings of inadequacy.

- Students can often overestimate how much time they have to do a task in and underestimate how long the task will actually take.

- They will often also choose to complete an interesting or fun activity, both as a way to gain some immediate pleasure and as a way of avoiding or escaping the non-preferred task.

To help with this EF skill teachers need to model and encourage pupils to make the overwhelming jobs more manageable, by breaking them down into separate chunks or tasks, and tackling one task at a time. Pupils will need this demonstrated to them repeatedly before they have the skills themselves to be able to do this.

The following checklist will help teachers gauge how well they support task initiation in the classroom.

TEACHER SELF-REVIEW CHECKLIST: TASK INITIATION

I support students' difficulties with task initiation by:	Yes	No
Putting instructions on the whiteboard so pupils can work through them		
Breaking bigger tasks down into smaller ones		
Modelling how to answer questions		
Minimising distractions in the classroom		
Making the lesson as engaging as possible		
Teaching planning and organisation		
Providing guidance on / modelling how to prioritise work		
Setting time limits to complete tasks in, so that pupils know they are time-limited		
Using timers to show the passage of time and the countdown of time		
My own ideas...		

Ways you can model and support students to develop and support their own task initiation skills

- Be clear about your instructions and what you expect; use visual reminders.

- For those who need it, provide one small thing to get them started rather than expecting them to be able to break the tasks down themselves.

- Provide / model how to break a task down by using written 'to do' lists to help students begin an activity – striking off the steps can help generate a sense of achievement, reframing their sense of achievement.

- To help pupils improve their task avoidance, you will need to model and promote their self-talk, so that they can overcome obstacles and knuckle down and get going. You will need to encourage them to engage in an internal conversation. If you are able to model this to them when setting tasks, it will help them to learn the process. This could be along the lines of:

  > This is the first step; all I need to do is start.

  > I will just start with...[a small chunk of the whole task].

  > I will work for [a defined amount of time].

  > If I don't take this step, I won't get any closer to finishing / achieving my goal.

  > I can ask for help if I need.

  > If I don't understand what I am being asked to do, I can ask someone to explain it to me.

  Often if you can break down the barrier to just getting started, a bit of momentum builds and the pupil can work a bit longer than they thought – and if they cannot, they go through the process again, for the next chunk of the task.

Classroom ideas for teachers to help with task initiation

- For some pupils prompting (both verbal and non-verbal) may be necessary to help them get started – stop by a pupil's desk at the outset of each task and prompt them to start work or perhaps demonstrate the first problem of a worksheet.

- Rather than viewing some pupils as unmotivated, try to reframe it as a task initiation difficulty that can be supported and overcome.

- Peers can often help to model good task initiation; working in pairs and small groups can encourage those pupils who find this area difficult, as interaction with peers will continuously act as a prompt.

- Difficulties with initiating are often a problem of not knowing where to start. Provide structure and examples to help to demonstrate where to begin and what steps to follow.

- As with any executive difficulty, it can be helpful to increase pupils' awareness of their difficulty in the area of initiation. As they become more metacognitively aware of their own challenges getting started, they become more proactive in using the strategies more actively.

- Some teachers might also find it useful to get students to go through a formal process of self-reflection by completing a checklist that reflects on their feedback and what went well by asking them to use a self-assessment scale, ranging from achieving more than they expected through to less than expected, and asking them to record why this might be.

- Some pupils benefit from setting time goals to help them to get started and to complete tasks. Using a visual timer helps keep them on track.

- Discuss the obstacles to achieving long-term goals with the pupils and help them to develop ways to overcome those obstacles by developing interim goals.

- Talk to pupils about how they feel when they get straight on with a task (good feelings) and how they feel when a task hangs over them and they put it off (bad feelings). Discuss with them that they can take ownership of those feelings and be in control of them, if they can learn good task initiation skills.

- If a task seems overwhelming, encourage the pupil to break the task down into more manageable parts, with specific deadlines for each. By simplifying the task and reducing the steps by breaking the task down into parts, each with a reduced number of steps that go to make up the whole, this will make them more explicit and easier to achieve.

- Try to encourage them to make an explicit plan for when / how the task will get done. This will provide them with more owner-ship and control over the process, and can positively affect their ability to get started. Encouraging them to break the task down into small steps will make it seem more manageable.

- Prioritise what needs to get done by making a task list / daily 'to do' list; for older learners consider discussing with them that they can set reminders on their phone and use apps to help them.

- Where possible try to let the pupil decide on deadlines and queueing systems that work best for them in order to trigger a willingness to engage in task initiation.

- Trying to stay positive will help with the pupil engaging more with task initiation.

- Either sensitively allocate or encourage pupils to get an 'account-ability partner' to hold them accountable for tasks that they say they will do.

- Encourage the pupil to understand that once they get started on a task, if they get into the flow of it, they should keep on working and maximise their 'flow state', so that more of the task gets completed.

- Pupils could be encouraged to set themselves their own rewards for completing certain tasks, although they would need guidance about what those rewards might look like and how they need to be sensible and attainable.

- Talk to pupils about tracking how much time they waste on pro-crastination, so that they can conceptualise how much time they might have to do other, better things, if they can master their task initiation skills.

- At the end of the task give feedback to assist internalisation and generalisation of their approaches, by sensitively indicating dis-crepancies between the pupil's work and the desired product, so that they can see how they can make their work even better.

- Peer coaching can also be a useful resource as long as care is taken in teaming the pupils with each other, so that the relationship is productive and the pupils are able to help each other to get started – possibly by employing a range of these strategies.

- Plot the task end date on a calendar and work out the timescale, and chunk the task into smaller, more manageable, tasks, building up to the deadline.

Resources

Provide structured feedback to students

Feedback should help pupils to understand how to improve by helping them to internalise and generalise their approach:

- Sensitively indicate discrepancies between the pupil's work and the desired product, so that they can see how they can make their work even better.

- For those who struggled with task initiation, the feedback may include explicit reference to this, with gentle encouragement that next time, if they were able to use their time more efficiently and effectively, they could achieve even higher marks.

- Drawing a pupil's attention to the correlation between difficulties in initiating what needs to be done and reducing the available time they have to spend on the task will highlight the importance of developing their own task initiation strategies.

- Highlight that having strategies to overcome task initiation difficulties will help them to reduce their frustration and the risk of mismanaging the situation and missing deadlines etc.

Encourage students to identify their own procrastination difficulties

Brainstorm procrastination triggers

Help pupils to identify task initiation difficulties (for non-preferred tasks) to help increase their self-awareness of what their possible triggers are, by discussing with them, and encouraging them to self-reflect about:

- What they avoid and why – are there some common themes, i.e., regular or reoccurring events or tasks that they avoid?

- Whether they put off homework or chores until the last minute?

- Whether it is hard for them to put aside fun activities to start schoolwork?

- Whether they need lots of reminders to start activities?

Try to encourage them to identify and name distractors that prevent them from getting started. Then identify strategies and ways they will overcome this. If they find it difficult to think of some strategies, you could suggest any of the following – but they need to take ownership of it, so encourage them to discuss *how* they would use the strategies they select:

- Keep tasks small and manageable, breaking a big project into multiple, smaller steps.

- Set a timer.

- Set a stopping point.

- Figure out what to do – focus on rewards, not punishments.

- Try to make it more fun.

- Create a reward when one doesn't otherwise exist.

- Shorten the wait for rewards and punishments.

- Use your energy bursts productively.

- Remind yourself of how you would like to see yourself.

- Just jump in and get going.

Encourage self-talk

Procrastination is the enemy of planning and prioritisation. Encourage pupils to ask themselves:

- What are the main causes of my procrastination?

- What kind of things distract me and prevent me from getting started on something?

- Are there rewards that might motivate me that I might be able to realise?

Pupils can use the following worksheet to increase their self-awareness of what their possible triggers are.

WORKSHEET: INCREASING TASK INITIATION ABILITIES (FOR NON-PREFERRED TASKS)

Things I avoid	Yes / no	My comments
I find it hard to get started on tasks in class		
I find it hard to get started on homework		
I avoid things that will require effort or hard work		
I find other smaller tasks to do than starting a big project		
I find it hard to break tasks down into smaller chunks		
Anything else / your own ideas...		

The following are some self-help strategies for pupils. Being able to make yourself start a task if you've seen yourself getting closer to your goal is the first step on that path. If you don't take this step, you cannot get closer.

Tips	Self-talk
Pick the task (make it small)	Just do it
Pick the start time	Take small steps
Pick the minimum work time	Start small
Pick the cue to start	
Other strategies:	**Your own idea(s):**

TWINK

- **T**hink about the task.

- **W**rite three steps to begin the task:

  - ....

  - ....

  - ....

- **I**nitiate (begin) the first step.

- **N**ext step – begin the next step.

- **K**eep on going.

Source: Taken from Moyes (2014, p.84)

FOR PUPILS WHO PARTICULARLY STRUGGLE WITH TASK INITIATION

- For those pupils who find it really hard to find the internal drive and self-motivation for things that they really do not want to do and that really hold no personal interest for them, encourage them to create a reason to complete the task – this might be that it will make you (their teacher) or their parent happy. Discourage negative incentives, such as avoidance of punishment, because then the task feels punitive and has a negative connotation – and may therefore even encourage the procrastination. If the pupil can feel positive about it – even if it is to please someone else – this is a better mindset to be fostering.

- For those pupils who are emotionally distracted, with either high or low feelings, help them to know how to manage this type of distraction by working with them to use breathing techniques to control the emotion to the point where they can engage in the task. Encouraging them to take approximately 2–3 minutes to take deep breaths, and to empty their minds by having their eyes closed and focusing on their breathing, may help them to prepare for the task in hand.

CHAPTER 9

Sustained Attention

EF skill	Explanation	Classroom impact
Sustained attention	The ability to focus and pay attention, even if the task is not very engaging	• Difficulty following through and being able to complete a task without supervision or external pressure to complete it • Starting something and not finishing it • In class finding it hard to work for the required period without distraction

What is sustained attention?

Sustained attention is the capacity to keep focusing on a situation or task in hand despite distractions, fatigue or boredom.

From an educational point of view this means being able to maintain attention in class and persevere with homework. If a pupil's sustained attention is weak, you will be conscious that they may need directions / instructions to be repeated frequently, or that they are regularly 'off task'. You may also be aware of a pupil jumping, or 'grasshopping', from one task to another and often failing to complete the preceding task before choosing to move on to a second. This is less obvious perhaps in a school setting, but at home, that same child may look for distractions, such as checking their phone every few minutes, and fail to complete homework tasks; alternatively, you may get reports from home that the set work is taking a very long time for the child to complete each evening.

It should be noted that, as a generation, it is possible that our children have less capacity for sustained attention than previous generations, in part because of the fast-paced technological world in which they live, where things seem designed for instant gratification rather than persistence and perseverance.

What you might see in a pupil who struggles with sustained attention

- They appear to be easily externally distracted by things in their environment – e.g., looking out of the window or being distracted by noises or activities in the classroom or corridor.

- They are internally distracted – e.g., lost in their own thoughts.

- They need to take regular breaks when working.

- They find it hard to regulate the length of their breaks and therefore take breaks that are too long.

- They take breaks too frequently.

- They run out of steam before they have finished.

- They do not recognise for themselves when they are 'off task'.

- They find it hard to follow instructions.

- They make careless errors in their written work.

Some of the things you will need to discuss with pupils and encourage them to think about

- Is it more difficult to sustain attention with some subjects than others?

- What kind of internal conversation are they having with themselves that leads them to either give up or to stick with it?

- Does the length of the piece of work make a difference to their ability to complete it?

It will also be important for you to help pupils to identify the following:

- What kinds of things distract them?

- Is there an environment / workspace that minimises their distractions?

- How do they manage the distractions when they occur?

Once you have been able to raise their awareness of these points, you can then go on to help them by:

- Setting realistic work goals and encouraging them to stick to them

- Establishing when to take planned breaks and then getting back to work on schedule

- Encouraging them to get into the routine of gathering all necessary materials before beginning a task, so that there are no obstacles and distractions to hinder progress once they have started.

You will need to help promote the concept of working first and then playing / resting etc. afterwards. If you are able to help pupils to build in their own personal rewards for completing tasks (in the class this could be the opportunity to chat to a neighbour for 2 minutes, and at home it could be a short stint on social media for completing something), this will build their ability and independence at taking control of their attention and focus.

The Pomodoro Technique[1] is a popular method of working where worktime is broken into 25-minute chunks with 5-minute breaks, with the cycle being repeated. It is important to remember that they will need help until they learn the routine, and that once the reward is over, they then need to get back to work.

The following checklist will help teachers gauge how well they support sustained attention in the classroom.

---

1   www.pomodorotechnique.com/what-is-the-pomodoro-technique.php

TEACHER SELF-REVIEW CHECKLIST: SUSTAINED ATTENTION

I support students' sustained attention by:	Yes	No
Reinforcing and praising good examples of focus and attention		
Breaking bigger tasks down into smaller ones		
Using timers to count down how long a task will take		
Minimising distractions in the classroom		
Making the lesson as engaging as possible		
Consistently using the same key phrases to engage pupils' attention		
Making my teaching as multisensory – e.g., visual and verbal – as possible		
Being aware who might have particular challenges in this area and using preferential seating to help them		
My own ideas...		

Ways you can model and support students to develop their sustained attention

- Always give praise for staying on task and for successfully completing a task (instead of negative connotations, e.g., avoid pupils perceiving that you 'nag' them to get work done).

Classroom ideas for teachers to help with sustained attention difficulties

- Try to minimise distractions in the classroom environment.

- Try to encourage pupils to identify particular tasks (e.g., homework) that are tough for them to sustain their focus on; talk to them about whether there are ways to modify the tasks (such as breaking them into smaller parts) that would help them to maintain attention and complete the task.

- Ensure pupils know what they are required to do, and where possible back this up in writing – a checklist is ideal, as pupils know they need to work through it.

- Provide supervision, by checking in with pupils at regular intervals to see how they are doing, or to help them put the distractions to one side.

- Develop pupils' self-awareness about how long they can work on a task before needing a break; consider whether the regular use of a timer for certain activities would be a good idea to depict the passing of time and to indicate the end point of the task (children often can have a distorted sense of the passage of time, particularly if it is a task they are reluctant to do).

- Use incentive systems, e.g., 'first...then' plans, whereby they complete the less preferred activity first and can then move on to a more preferred one.

- Encourage pupils to consider the environment in which they work best, and to make sensible choices about who they sit next to, to minimise distractions.

Resources

The following worksheet will help pupils increase their self-awareness of what their possible triggers are.

WORKSHEET: MANAGING SUSTAINED ATTENTION

My challenges	Yes / no	My comments
I get easily distracted by things in my environment, e.g., looking out of the window or being distracted by noises or activities in the classroom or corridor		
I get easily internally distracted and get lost in my own thoughts		
I need to take regular breaks when working		
I find it hard to regulate the length of my breaks, and take breaks that are too long		
I take breaks too frequently		
I often run out of steam before I have finished		
I am not really aware if I am off task or not		
Anything else / your own ideas...		

This worksheet can then be developed and extended by coupling it with the one below.

EXTENSION – SELF-REFLECTION WORKSHEET

Related questions	My answers
What kind of things distract you?	
Do you find it harder to hold your focus in some subjects than others?	
Why might this be?	
What could you do to help change this?	
Does the length of the piece of work make a difference in your ability to complete it?	
Do you have any strategies that work for you that help to keep you focused?	
What are they? Are there certain environments / spaces / places where you can focus better than others? Where are they?	

Here are some self-help strategies for pupils.

Tips	Self-talk
Set realistic work goals and stick to them	You cannot walk away from this
Take planned breaks and get back to work on schedule	Don't quit now
Gather all necessary materials before beginning a task Build in rewards for completing tasks	Back to work Work first, then play
Other strategies:	**Your own idea(s):**

Pupils can build on the TWINK technique introduced in Chapter 8 by adding some strategies to build sustained attention, as highlighted by the use of italics.

TWINK

- Think about the task.

- Write three steps to begin the task:

  – . . . .

  – . . . .

  – . . . .

- Initiate (begin) the first step.

- Next step – begin the next step.

- Keep on going.

Source: Taken from Moyes (2014, p.85)

GOOD APPS TO HELP PUPILS WITH THEIR SUSTAINED ATTENTION

- OneTab[2] helps students to organise their browser tabs into lists and categories, as well as hiding the distracting ones.

- Pomofocus[3] – like Pomodoro, this app includes a timer for 25 minutes of sustained work.

- BlockSite[4] is a website and app blocker, to block distractions while the pupil works.

- Flora[5] – use this app to grow virtual trees. For some reason pupils seem to really buy into the idea of growing 'forests' and not letting their trees die by resisting using any other media while engaged in a period of work.

---

2   www.one-tab.com
3   www.pomofocus.io
4   https://blocksite.co
5   https://flora.appfinca.com/en

FOR THOSE PUPILS WHO NEED ADDITIONAL, MORE FOCUSED SUPPORT WITHIN THE CLASSROOM

- Consider whether your expectations of the pupils you teach suits the sustained attention of those with a shorter attention span in class, and whether you can make any adaptations to help them, that might help the class more generally by cutting down on any disruptions that may ensue once the pupil(s) are off track and have lost focus. Adopting an approach such as the Pomodoro Technique – or your version of it, that suits your subject and the work requirements of the task in hand – could benefit the pupils once the routine of using it was established (particularly if accompanied by a visual count-down stopwatch) because they would be able to predict when the next short break is, and could visually track the passage of time they need to work for, until being able to pause and refocus.

- Consider agreeing a discreet signal you can give the pupil to signify that you are aware they are off task, to encourage them to get back on task.

- Depending on the school rules and the class set-up, consider whether you are happy for those pupils who need them to wear noise-cancelling headphones.

- Break the work down into smaller segments with a tick list so that the pupil moves through smaller sections of work and feels success by ticking off the completed tasks.

- Provide cognitive breaks where the pupil is allowed to take a short break from what they are doing, before re-engaging with it.

- Consider whether the pupil works better with a 'concentrator' (otherwise known as a fidget tool), and if so, consider agreeing that they can use it, providing they are discreet with it.

CHAPTER 10

Goal-Directed Persistence

EF skill	Explanation	Classroom impact
Goal-directed persistence	The ability to meet targets and goals, by sticking at it until finished	• Difficulty with persisting at something • Giving up on things • Finding it hard to complete a project / persist with revision

What is goal-directed persistence?

Goal-directed persistence is the ability to set a goal and pursue its achievement. It requires the pupil to have an understanding that how they behave today has consequences that may impact later achievements. This is thought to be the last EF to mature, and it can continue to develop as late as into someone's mid-twenties.

Those pupils with poor goal-directed persistence will tend to focus their attention on the here and now and find the concept of future goals difficult to visualise. Therefore, we need to teach goal setting, and students need to know why and how to develop this life-long skill. The school environment provides a good opportunity to develop pupils' concept of persistence through different means – such as through sport, practising playing an instrument, persisting learning times tables etc. – to achieve a goal. It also promotes the concept of delaying instant gratification to work on something more important.

Pupils should be encouraged to become less reliant on external motivation (deadlines imposed by teachers, avoidance of sanctions etc.) towards an internal motivation where they have their own sense of purpose and desire to achieve.

What you might see in pupils with poor goal-directed persistence

- They live in the 'now', with little awareness of future aspirations or consequences.
- They have no idea of what they want to achieve or where they want to go with their future plans.
- They find it hard to stick to a routine and follow something through.
- They do not complete things.

The following checklist will help teachers gauge how well they support goal-directed persistence in the classroom.

TEACHER SELF-REVIEW CHECKLIST:
GOAL-DIRECTED PERSISTENCE

I support students' goal-directed persistence by:	Yes	No
Modelling setting long- and short-term (academic) goals		
Setting SMART goals explicitly so pupils become familiar with them		
Breaking tasks down into smaller, achievable tasks		
Focusing on process and progress rather than outcomes		
Resisting from stepping in too early or too frequently and allowing pupils to 'work it out'		
Stepping in, supporting and re-engaging the pupil at the point when they seem to have come to a full stop		
My own ideas...		

Ways you can model and support students to develop their own goal-directed persistence

- A good way to demonstrate goal-directed persistence to a class is via the way you structure and manage your lesson, because by stating the learning objectives at the beginning of the lesson you will be setting out the framework of what content needs to be covered. This will allow you to reflect with the class at the end whether those objectives have been met, and if not, to demonstrate flexibility by verbalising to the class how it can be fitted into the structure of the next lesson.

- If you can operate a consistent routine at the beginning of each lesson, then, once the learning objectives have been highlighted, the class will know the direction the lesson will take.

- It is your task as the teacher to move the class towards achieving those objectives or goals. You may choose to do this by modelling how to break down the general learning objectives into smaller, achievable steps:

  - Sometimes lessons will not entirely take the direction planned, because of external events that interrupt it, or because the discussion (controlled by you) takes an interesting and worthwhile (hopefully minor) diversion from what was planned.

  - If, or when, this happens it is worth highlighting to pupils and explaining how you plan to make sure the goal set at the beginning of the lesson will be achieved in the future, e.g., in the next lesson.

- Your role as the teacher is to provide:

- Consistency in the repetition of tasks

- Positive reinforcement for good strategies – it has to be meaningful

- A positive approach yourself.

- By using the language in class of goal setting and pursuing goals, and how you anticipate interruptions and deal with barriers to achieving goals, you will help to model and develop a growth mindset, resilience and perseverance.

- Focus on progress, not results.

- Acknowledge and celebrate small milestones.

Classroom ideas for teachers to help with goal-directed persistence

- The principal teaching goal here is for students to understand:

  - The benefit of goal setting – short, medium and long term

  - How to set goals

  - How to go about achieving them

  - How to predict and overcome challenges

  - How to track progress.

- Goal setting – understanding the difference between long-, medium- and short-term goals:

  - You can help pupils to understand the difference between the types of goals by using explicit language when talking about their curriculum.

  - You can identify with them what the long-term goals are, i.e., what the curriculum overview is for that academic year in your subject.

  - You can also identify medium-term goals – what you plan to cover over the term.

- And short-term goals – what you will cover in the week or the lesson.

This will help pupils to see that short-term goals can be part of a larger project, but also, that some short-term goals can be separate and distinct from other longer-term goals, and can be set and achieved in small amounts of time.

How to help pupils set goals

In terms of pupils beginning to understand their own abilities to set goals and achieve them, they need to understand how to break larger goals into smaller, achievable steps:

- Encourage pupils to track their progress with checklists so that they get into the habit of frequently checking that they are on task.

- Consider whether getting pupils to identify short- and medium-term targets is sensible in your subject / classroom – it can be a good motivator for those who cannot yet find their internal motivation.

- When being encouraged to set goals, pupils should be helped to understand the difference between dreams and achievable goals. This can be done, in part, by the concept of being able to set SMART targets to achieve goals (specific, measurable, attainable, relevant and time-bound). We improve our chances of achieving our goals by writing them down and being able to review them. We need to be able to describe why the goal is important so it has relevance and meaning. How will they know when they have achieved their goal? What will success look like for them?

How to predict and overcome challenges

- We can help to promote the benefit of good routines with students by identifying struggles they might face, be it pessimism, avoidance, anxiety, procrastination and spending time on activities that give much more instant gratification and feedback. These can hijack their goals.

How to go about achieving goals

- We can encourage students to think of ways that they can keep their goals live and real, so that they have reminders of what they are striving for. They will need to understand the different types of goals that they might set themselves: the ones about what they want to achieve in life and other goals about how they want to develop as people. But we also need to encourage them to think of school-based assignments, tests and tasks as worthy goals to strive to be successful in as well.

- In terms of school-based goals, they can be encouraged to think of what incentives might help to motivate them and what strategies might help them with their persistence – such as the use of alarms and the reminder facility on phones to complete work.

- Different goals are needed for different types of tasks, e.g., homework that might be due in tomorrow or for a long-term project not due in for half a term. The longer-term project requires goals that are slightly more complex than the obvious goal of 'Do my homework'. For the project they need to be able to see or visualise the overview of what it requires and what it will look like, then they need to be able to break it down into component parts or chunks and set a time frame. Pupils should be encouraged to set mini goals within the larger project.

- Pupils can also be encouraged to set longer-term aspirational goals to motivate them that are not associated with school. They can think about the people who inspire them to achieve their goals, and you could ask them to find some motivational quotes to help them to achieve their goals.

- Encourage pupils not to set goals that are too far into the future. Help them to identify and set shorter-term goals that might help them achieve those longer-term ones and that help to reinforce the ultimate goal.

- Teachers can use a more generalised / non-school-focused concept of goal setting to trigger conversations within the class that achieving goals works best through internal motivation rather than from external pressure, as they will probably more readily make the link when it involves their personal aspirations.

- To be successful, the pupil needs to have the desire to achieve internally – not because of an external pressure.

- They will need to find ways to explore and tap into this and will need to find their own motivations.

- It will also help them to understand that goals can give us structure and direction, ambition and achievement.

This can trigger conversations about positive role models pupils could identify with who can be used as mentors / motivators. It can also be used to instil an understanding that practice generates success – perhaps by using the elite athlete as a sports analogy – and repeated practice is needed to succeed, not just natural flare.

This more generalised focus on aspirational goal setting can then be brought back to the business of school and education, and the same principles apply:

- Educational success requires time, practice and effort – it is not about natural flair.

- It is important to establish a goal and carry it through to completion.

- This requires being able to resist getting distracted by other interests.

- It will require pupils to think about and identify obstacles that might get in their way.

- Anticipating exams and tests reinforces that practice – practising questions etc. – will help bring about success.

- Encourage pupils to outline their SMART goals – breaking them down into smaller, achievable goals.

- Build in time for peer support and accountability sessions for pupils to check in with each other.

- Encourage a growth mindset that the goals are attainable with application and some hard work.

How to track progress

- Progress can be tracked and monitored through completing checklists and looking back on the short-, medium- and long-term goals and ticking off achievements.

Resources

Here are some pupil-focused activities. The first is a checklist for pupils to record their goals and ambitions for their future self.

GOAL-DIRECTED PERSISTENCE CHECKLIST

- Make the tasks small and achievable.
- If starting or persisting is hard, consider using a timer.
- Give yourself a stop time.
- Try to make it fun and enjoyable.
- Consider what the rewards might be for completing tasks.
- Consider how your future self would talk to you now about achieving the goals to succeed in life.
- Learn from setbacks.

GOAL SETTING PLAN OF ACTION

1. Come up with a short-, medium- and long-term goal.
2. Discuss and identify the steps needed to complete each.
3. Create checklists to support the goals.
4. Identify what you need to achieve the goals, i.e., the tools.

5. Identify the timescale.

6. Identify the steps to success.

7. Identify the things that may make achieving the goals difficult.

The process of working through this kind of checklist can help students to keep track of the goals and steps required. It can also help you to review it with them so that they can see what has worked / gone well and how realistic their goals were, and how to improve their setting and achieving of goals.

Goal [project title, title of essay, personal development goal etc.]:

Is it a short- or long-term goal?

Set a time limit [project deadline, submission date, when you want to have achieved a personal development goal]:

List the steps you need to do to complete the goal:

. . . .

. . . .

Put a date you hope to achieve each step:

If I go off track I will help myself get back on track by [list some self-help strategies]:

. . . .

. . . .

If I need assistance I can ask:

I will know I have achieved my goal when:

I will feel...

TEACHER CHECKLIST: GOAL SETTING FOR PRIMARY SCHOOLCHILDREN

- Set goals that are achievable within the day.
- Build up to larger goals.
- Build in rewards.
- Increase time needed to spend on goals.
- Establish reminders to keep children focused, motivated and on task.
- Create visuals / charts to show this.
- Make targets SMART.
- Keep practising these skills.

GOAL PLANNING

List your goals:

....

....

....

Identify strategies to achieve them:

....

....

....

Set down the next steps:

....

....

....

Review

Did you complete the next steps?

What steps remain? [list them]

. . . .

. . . .

. . . .

. . . .

. . . .

WORKSHEET: WHY YOU DIDN'T ACHIEVE YOUR GOALS

Did you list your goals and identify what you needed to do, i.e., make them real and attainable?

Can you identify why you didn't achieve them – external or internal distractions?

. . . .

. . . .

. . . .

Can you identify any trends with other goals you might not have achieved?

. . . .

. . . .

. . . .

Are these trends something you can change in order to achieve success?

. . . .

. . . .

. . . .

How can you become accountable to make sure you hit your targets?

. . . .

. . . .

. . . .

WORKSHEET: GETTING READY FOR LEARNING AND ACHIEVING MY GOALS

What are things in your workspace that you've noticed interfere with your concentration?

. . . .

. . . .

. . . .

Is your workspace cluttered or organised?

. . . .

What steps can you take to change your workspace for better concentration? [break it down into a list]

. . . .

. . . .

. . . .

FOR THOSE PUPILS WHO NEED ADDITIONAL, MORE FOCUSED SUPPORT WITHIN THE CLASSROOM

- Encourage them to think back about goals they have already achieved.

- Ask them to consider how it made them feel.

- Discuss with them how the goals were achieved.

- Identify what worked well and what strategies they used.

- Encourage them to use those strategies again.

- Get them to identify what did not work well and why.

- How can they avoid those hiccups again?

- Break tasks down into SMART targets with them / for them to achieve their short-term goals.

CHAPTER 11

Planning and Prioritisation

EF skill	Explanation	Classroom impact
Planning and prioritisation	The ability to plan how to achieve a desired goal / outcome and to prioritise the steps needed to achieve it	• Difficulty knowing how / where to start on a task • Difficulty in having an idea of the steps you need to go through to complete a project • Not knowing how to plan an essay

What is planning and prioritisation?

While Chapter 10 explored goal setting, this chapter will look at how to plan to achieve the desired goal, and how to prioritise the attainment of that goal by focusing on what is most important and not getting distracted or diverted by smaller, less relevant things along the way.

Having set a goal, the EF skill of planning and prioritisation helps with the roadmap to achieve the goal – short-term goals are easier to 'see' and achieve than longer-term goals, and so pupils need to learn to break long-term goals down into smaller ones, with specific steps to follow.

Planning and prioritisation go hand in hand and are interlinked with organisation, as pupils need to be organised to succeed at planning and prioritisation.

What you might see in a pupil with poor planning and prioritisation

- Not making a study plan (not knowing how)

- Not being able to break larger tasks into smaller ones and rank them in importance

- Not being able to come up with timelines to complete things

- Missing deadlines and due dates

- Not having the foresight to take detailed notes to study from

- Taking too many notes and not knowing how to detect important from unimportant facts

- Spending too much time on less important elements – finding it difficult to put the most important jobs first

- Being unrealistic with plans

- Difficulty determining what is important

- Not being able to visualise what the completed task will look like.

The ability to develop a sense of time (see Chapter 13) is useful for planning and prioritisation because it helps to create perspective about where the project sits in terms of any deadlines, thus enabling the pupil to be able to plan back from that to come up with a plan of how to get to the desired outcome, factoring in opportunities for preview and review. Teachers need to be able to model this process as well as encouraging pupils to become internally motivated to complete a task, because ultimately the pupil will need to be able to set up their own system and timetable, and self-manage. By developing pupils' awareness of this skill, it will also help them to reflect about how they use their time and whether they use it effectively.

It is useful to regularly check in with pupils to see how they are getting on with their planning and prioritisation skills as they work towards a big project or an impending test.

The following checklist will help teachers gauge how well they support planning and prioritising in the classroom.

TEACHER SELF-REVIEW CHECKLIST:
PLANNING AND PRIORITISATION

I support students' planning and prioritisation by:	Yes	No
Ensuring they know what the goal is they need to achieve for a task		
Emphasising the importance of planning work – and modelling planning answers		
Discussing the most important steps of a task and recording them for pupils to follow		
Modelling a 'to do' list on the whiteboard and crossing off the tasks when completed		
Ensuring pupils accurately record homework deadlines, test dates etc.		
Providing a countdown to a test / homework deadline so that pupils are aware it is approaching		
Modelling planning techniques such as mind maps / other planning strategies		
My own ideas...		

Ways you can model and support students to develop their own planning and prioritisation skills

- Model how to plan tasks. Set out your planning process visually so that pupils can see it, as well as hearing you discuss how you would approach a task (there are examples of how to do this in the Resources section at the end of this chapter).

- Vocalise and provide guidance about your expectations, identifying what a successful end result looks like.

- When you are teaching or demonstrating how to do tasks, model phrases such as 'first, second, next, last' etc. so that pupils are used to hearing the language of order and structure.

- Model how to start small by breaking things down. Planning helps to break down large, possibly overwhelming tasks into smaller chunks.

- Model the order of events, i.e., identify what needs to come first / what things need to happen before other steps are started.

- Model when you are giving instructions for tasks and projects how to underline and number each instruction so that it becomes an action to be completed.

- Talk to students about energy levels – identify your best energy time zone (morning / evening etc.) and explain that this is when you are at your optimal point for learning and working, so that they can begin to self-reflect and develop their awareness about their own energy levels.

- Use timers, alarms and reminders about lesson start / end / tasks, so that students can learn they are time-limited.

Classroom ideas for teachers to help with planning and prioritisation difficulties

- Encourage students to brainstorm / make a list of ideas on paper to reduce the load on their working memory. They can then number and prioritise their ideas, before turning it into a more formal plan of action.

- Encourage students to plan, and model the planning process as much as possible when guiding them through tasks and work expectations.

- Motivate how to get started on tasks and prioritise the order to do something by asking students to identify what needs to get done as the first step, next step, and so on in the process.

- Encourage students to break the task into smaller, more manageable segments.

- Have a discussion about 'What you can do to help you stick to your plan'.

- Make sure students understand clearly what your expectations are for a completed task.

- Encourage students to make a (mental) note of the order in which the tasks need to be completed – what comes first, next, next, and what do they need to do to get there?

- Keep checking in with students to make sure they are on track.

- Encourage students to create 'planning forms' to help keep them on track.

- Identify the most important points and concepts to focus on when telling students to study for a test / producing a project.

- Set time limits for certain tasks and use timers and alarms, so that students develop a sense of the passage of time.

Resources

Resources to help with planning and prioritisation include:

- Creating checklists

- Daily planners

- Using technology, e.g.:

  - Apps that help to block distractions (such as Forest[1])

  - The Pomodoro Technique[2] / app that promotes set periods of work and rest

---

1   www.forestapp.cc
2   www.pomodorotechnique.com/what-is-the-pomodoro-technique.php

- Using time trackers – stopwatch / alarm function / time tracking apps

- Using a calendar on the phone to set and track task due dates

- Project planners

- Scheduling tasks on a visual planner

- Free graphic organisers, such as Freeology.[3]

WORKSHEET: IDENTIFYING TASKS AND DUE DATES

What do I need to do? (List each step in order)	When will I do it?	Tick when done
1.		
2.		
3.		
4.		

REMINDER LIST

Include here any additional tasks or details you need to keep in mind as you work. Cross out or check each one off as you do it
1.
2.

3   www.freeology.com

3.

4.

5.

6.

7.

DAILY REMINDERS – THINGS I CANNOT FORGET

Monday	Tuesday	Wednesday	Thursday	Friday	Saturday	Sunday

FOR THOSE PUPILS WHO NEED ADDITIONAL, MORE FOCUSED SUPPORT WITHIN THE CLASSROOM

- **Enco**urage them to think back about goals they have already achieved.

- Ask them to consider how it made them feel.

- Discuss with them how were they achieved.

- Identify what worked well and what strategies they used.

- Encourage them to use those strategies again.

- Get them to identify what did not work well and why?

- How can they avoid those hiccups again?

- Break tasks down into SMART targets with them / for them to achieve their short-term goals.

CHAPTER 12

Organisation

EF skill	Explanation	Classroom impact
Organisation	The ability to have a well-ordered mind and to be neat, tidy and methodical with possessions and workspaces	• Messy, chaotic school bag • Disorganised notes • Difficulty finding things

What is organisation?

Organisation is the ability to have systems and strategies to keep track of important information and things.

What we are trying to teach students via this EF skill is that having a reasonably organised work environment (and when at home, an organised bedroom / homework place) increases efficiency by eliminating the need to waste lots of time looking for things, which, in turn, reduces stress.

The concept of organisation also applies to written work and having an organised and logical order to it.

What you might see in a pupil who has poor organisational skills

- They have a messy, poorly organised school bag.

- They have a messy, poorly organised workspace / desk.

- They have an untidy locker.

- They lose things or forget where they have been left.

- They do not know how to organise / set out a written piece of work.

- They do not know how to save electronic work in a logical manner with an effective filing system.

What good organisational skills may look like

- A tidy desk, locker, bag, exercise book – where the pupil can find things when they need them.

- Making numbers and calculations orderly and easy to follow in maths, well set out science and geographical formulae, diagrams etc.

- Being able to write essays and longer answers so that their ideas on one topic are all in one section or paragraph.

The following checklist will help teachers gauge how well they promote organisation in the classroom.

TEACHER SELF-REVIEW CHECKLIST: ORGANISATION

I support students' organisation by:	Yes	No
Clearly labelling, dating and putting headings on my handouts		
Writing the homework task on the whiteboard, and giving my students long enough to copy it accurately		
Setting out notes on the whiteboard in a coherent, organised and logical order that students can follow and copy easily		
Ensuring students highlight test dates in their planners		
My own ideas...		

It is important to remember:

- Different pupils, and in particular neurodivergent children, may have different organisational methods and strategies, but the key is that they understand and can operate within their own systems.

- Teachers should encourage a strengths-based approach to encourage pupils to find their own system of organisation even though that might not look like what is typically thought of as 'organised', rather than impose set systems on them.

Ways you can model and support students to develop their own organisation skills

- Where possible, try to model some simple organisational operations. This could be verbalising that you are putting the due date for the homework you set in your own school diary so that you do not forget it, or modelling how to keep the classroom tidy and organised – you can involve the students in this process so that they learn organisational skills while doing this.

- Try to share examples from your own (professional) life that you are comfortable sharing.

- Establish a daily routine that you model to students.

- Use a digital planner or calendar on the interactive whiteboard to schedule upcoming class-based events and tasks so that students can observe how you do this and how it helps to keep you / them organised.

- Run a tidy, well organised classroom. Involve students in tidying the classroom before the end of the lesson.

Classroom ideas for teachers to help with organisation difficulties
In the short term it is sensible to offer pupils reminders about their organisation, even though your goal is to be able to withdraw those reminders in due course. However, transforming a pupil's skills in this area, in a short space of time, is unrealistic; they will need to be scaffolded and have strategies modelled to them, until they begin to adopt them independently.

Depending on the school's policy, pupils could be encouraged to use their phone / laptop to set reminders, or to use the latest apps to help with organisation.

Ideas for pupils to stay organised

- Have a system to store schoolwork – in folders or books depending on the subject requirements (show pupils how to organise their folders, e.g., colour coding and file dividers).

- Write any INCOMPLETE WORK in an organiser and keep a note in it of any tasks set, as soon as they are set, also noting the due date.

- Write the DUE DATE for tasks on the top of the task sheet itself as soon as you get it.

- As soon as you finish an assignment, mark it as completed, and file the completed work.

- Keep all work filed properly. Throw out pieces of paper that you do not have to keep – check if unsure.

- Have / develop a system for keeping work materials (such as pens, pencils, erasers, calculators etc.) tidy.

- Try to remove unnecessary items or clutter from their bag / workspace / bedroom at home.

- Get ready for things the night before (laying out clothes, getting ready for the next day's remote learning).

- Use memory aids (visual aids / checklists).

- Use visual reminders or a phone reminder.

- Try to observe what organised people do.

Strategies for computer organisation

- Keep everything in the same place, e.g., Google Drive / Google Classroom, Dropbox etc.

- Set up folders for each subject using proper names for them so that they are easily identifiable.

- Title each file and then file it in logical date order, as if it is being kept in the same way an exercise book is kept. Alternatively, store files in categories.

- Consider whether folders within folders are needed to store files in separate topics.

- It is essential to file immediately and not let a backlog develop as it becomes much harder to be systematic and there is a tendency to take short cuts.

- Back up work in the cloud.

Resources

The following student planning worksheet, or your own version of it, can be used in class for you to model how to plan and organise a piece of written work. Initially you should model completing it. After some iterations (for different pieces of work), then consider giving it to your pupils to complete on their own. You will need to continue to support how it is completed until you feel that your pupils are reaching an appropriate level of autonomy. Some will take longer to do this and will need the process repeated and modelled to them for an extended period. When you are confident that other pupils have developed some mastery, you could use peer support to help with this, but until then, you will need to provide ongoing (discreet) support for those in the class who need it.

WORKSHEET: STUDENT PLANNING

Title of task:

Subsections task can be broken into:

DUE DATE:

a. Subsection 1 target due date:

b. Subsection 2 target due date:

c. Subsection 3 target due date:

d. *Review date - on track?*

e. Subsection 1 target due date:

f. Subsection 2 target due date:

g. *Review and proofread date:*

SUBMISSION DATE:

FOR THOSE PUPILS WHO NEED ADDITIONAL, MORE FOCUSED SUPPORT WITHIN THE CLASSROOM

- Where possible, work collaboratively by engaging parents.

- Establish classroom routines – sticking work in exercise books, punching holes in them and filing them etc. Discreetly supervise that the pupil has completed this routine.

- Consider whether to keep hold of the pupil's exercise book / folder so that they have it for every lesson (rather than it being forgotten at home).

- Have personalised checklists for the pupil to work through to pack up / record homework / prepare to complete a task / desk tidiness etc.

- Allow extra time to record important information (homework etc.), or make sure you can provide a digital version of it, so that the pupil has it.

CHAPTER 13

Time Management

EF skill	Explanation	Classroom impact
Time management	The ability to understand the passage of time and an awareness of how long something will take Being aware of submission dates and deadlines	• Lack of punctuality, e.g., getting to lessons on time • Difficulty finishing schoolwork in a timely manner • Difficulty maintaining routines and deadlines • Difficulty working out how long something will take • Missing dates and deadlines

What is time management?

The concept of the passage of time is a very interesting one, and probably each of us has experienced a sense of time flying when we are enjoying ourselves and time dragging when we are not – and if this is so, then each of us has also had some sense of difficulty with time estimation. However, for the majority of us, that has hopefully been transient, and most of the time we have a relatively good sense of time. For some children, however, it is a really hard skill to master, be that because of age and stage of development, or because it is an EF that is challenging for them.

Time management is affected by other EF skills – task initiation, sustained attention, planning and prioritisation, and organisation. The most common misconception among pupils is how long something might take to do and therefore underestimating the time needed, thereby not planning and organising themselves effectively, and not initiating tasks in a timely manner. Sometimes, conversely, pupils will overestimate how long something will take, and this can then make the task seem overwhelming, so it becomes difficult to start, thereby making task initiation planning and organisation skills trickier to manage.

Time estimation and time management can be improved through practice. Encouraging pupils to estimate how long they think a task will take and then comparing it with how long it actually did take can highlight misconceptions between thoughts and practice. Getting pupils to track their time estimations over the term / year can help to improve their concept of time.

What you might see in a child who has poor time management skills

- Difficulty estimating how long a task will take – due to:
  - Overestimating how long it will take to do a task (therefore procrastinating to avoid starting)
  - Underestimating how long it will take to do a task (not prioritising and therefore running out of time)
  - Even if the above do not apply, still not finishing on time
- Being chronically late getting ready for school / obligations / appointments
- Difficulty juggling multiple tasks and responsibilities because they are not managing their time properly
- A lack of a sense of urgency / not appreciating that deadlines are important
- Relying on a deadline as an activator and motivator (and leaving things to the last minute in order to feel motivated by a very short deadline, to complete things)
- Trouble sticking to a timeline
- Problems estimating how long it will take to finish something (school-based tasks / homework)
- Putting off studying / not studying at all

- 'Wasting' time (e.g., hanging out with friends, playing computer games, social media, TV)

- Putting off doing homework at night and then rushing to get it done before class

- Being slow to get ready for things (school, appointments etc.)

- A lack of the sense of the passage of time.

The following checklist will help teachers gauge how well they promote time management in the classroom.

TEACHER SELF-REFLECTION CHECKLIST: TIME MANAGEMENT

I support students' time management by:	Yes	No
Having a clock clearly displayed on the wall (consider a digital clock to help those students who struggle to use an analogue clock)		
Using countdown timers clearly displayed (on an interactive whiteboard?) when pupils are completing independent tasks		
Having the day and date clearly displayed		
When setting tests, having the test date and a countdown of the days displayed somewhere in the classroom		
When setting a project, having a project timeline displayed		
My own ideas...		

Ways you can model and support students to develop their own time management skills

- Make a habit of checking the time regularly and expressing your inner voice to the pupils about the passage of time, so that they are alerted to it and it is modelled by you.

- Have the schedule or plan of the lesson visible for pupils to follow. Refer back to it and model this to them to show them you are checking it regularly and progressing through it. This will encourage pupils to get into the habit of doing this for themselves, regularly and habitually throughout the day, and help to develop their sense of the progression of the lesson.

- Model creating checklists and 'to do' lists that include start times and an estimate of how long things will take.

- Time how long things take in class so that it becomes part of the routine and pupils can begin to develop a sense of the passage of time.

- Have your own work-based 'to do' list on a small whiteboard that pupils can see you visibly mark off. Encourage pupils to keep their own 'to do' lists to manage expectations and help them to stay on task.

Classroom ideas for teachers to help with time management difficulties

Primary school classrooms typically tend to do a lot to assist with time management awareness in young pupils, because they often have a daily breakdown of the day displayed in the classroom, detailing the different lessons to be covered as well as having breaktimes and lunchtimes factored into the schedule, so that pupils get an overview of their day. This is a great tool to help children to track where they are in the progression of the day, and to develop a sense of time estimation. In addition, primary classroom teachers are often quite explicit with their task requirements, and, because of the young age of pupils, teachers usually break tasks down into achievable chunks.

- To further develop time management skills, teachers could consider whether the use of a countdown timer for each lesson is helpful, so that even if a daily plan has been displayed for pupils, they begin to hone their sense of time within each of the individual lessons / time slots allocated for different subjects.

- Schools could also consider whether a countdown timer / clock is appropriate outside the classroom, so that even during playtime and lunch, pupils can track the passage of time in a less structured environment, in free play, and begin to gauge for themselves when those free-time sessions start and finish.

- Games involving time also reinforce this skill.

By secondary school, pupils are often expected to have a developed sense of time – both the passing of time and time management. In reality, many pupils are not as au fait with this as might be expected. Many cannot use analogue clocks, and have a poor sense of time.

- Try to encourage pupils to become aware of school routines and their timings so as to develop a sense of the structure and passage of time of the school day.

- Consider having a countdown timer on display in each lesson, so that, within the context of the lesson plan (which has been displayed for pupils), they can begin to hone their sense of time within each of the individual lessons. Remind students when there are 5 minutes left.

- Encourage pupils when they are doing independent work / homework to set alarms or use apps or programs on phones etc. to help them get started on time.

- You can also help pupils to consider their time management away from school – at home – and the impact it has on schoolwork and their sense of success, e.g., encouraging them to avoid engrossing activities before they have tackled their essential work.

- Make a visual schedule / timetable and put it up in your classroom.

- Encourage pupils to reflect how much time they estimated for a task and to time how long it really took in reality. This will help them to understand the concept of over / underestimation of time linked to activities that they like / do not enjoy so much, as well as a general sense of the reality of the passage of time.

- You could also develop pupils' sense of time by removing access to all time-telling equipment and getting them to estimate the passage of time for a mix of different activities – fun, and more arduous. Repeating this from time to time will help to reinforce their sense of time.

- Encourage pupils to select a couple of time management tips that could help them, and to try them for a couple of weeks.

- Discuss with them whether they are going to enlist the help of someone – another pupil if it's time management in school, or perhaps a family member if it's time management at home – and consider how that person can hold them accountable.

- Also encourage the pupils to keep track of successes – for some this may be by physically recording it in a chart and to celebrate small gains, as well as considering why some strategies might not have worked and how they might be adjusted.

- The conclusion of this type of exercise would be to celebrate success and to review the positive impact good time keeping may have had on emotions and the successful management of other EF skills.

- For bigger projects pupils will need to have a sense of the whole project and how to break it into parts before they can get a sense of how time management will apply to the task. Encourage regular reviews of progress throughout the life of the project.

- Encourage pupils to use apps like the Pomofocus app[1] (#1 Time to focus!) for a customisable timer.

- Encourage pupils to use the technology on their phones, tablets or smartwatches to set alarms and reminders for homework.

---

[1]   https://pomofocus.io

Internal conversation / self-reflection

- Get pupils into the habit of regularly asking themselves what they should be doing now, so that they are developing habits of listening to their internal voice and creating self-reflective skills.

- Get pupils to reflect on how they feel when they are late – what emotions does it trigger?

- How does the pupil's time management impact others, and what emotions might that trigger in them?

- Ask pupils to visualise how they could change aspects of their lives and time keeping and also whether they can anticipate and visualise the obstacles that might occur to prevent them achieving their goals.

Resources

Effective external tools to encourage time management

- Wear a watch.

- Use stopwatches or countdown timers to set time limits for tasks.

- Use alarms to signal that a specific time has arrived.

- Use planners and a calendar to plan and prioritise tasks and plan out the time needed to do tasks. Do a chart of how you spend your time including sleep, exercise, school, social time, family time.

- Pomodoro is an app that can help with breaking tasks into segments; other apps are also available.

- Put up signs – motivational or instructional – to encourage pupils to stay on track and on time.

- Older learners can be encouraged to use browser add-ons to limit their online time on their phones or laptops.

WORKSHEET: TIME MANAGEMENT

When working through this worksheet if you feel you are good at the skill identified, tick the 'not a problem' box. If, however, it is an area you feel you need to tackle, record your thoughts (maybe why you find it tricky / how you might try to practice improvement) in the 'notes' section.

Item	Not a problem	Notes
I have trouble sticking to a timeline		
I often have problems estimating how long it will take to finish something (school-based tasks / homework)		
I put off studying / not studying at all		
I 'waste' time (e.g., hanging out with friends, playing computer games, social media, watching TV)		
I put off doing homework at night and rush to get it done before class		
I am slow to get ready for things (school, appointments etc.)		
Other ideas...		

Here are some self-help strategies for pupils.

Tips	Self-talk
Use a planner to make daily plans	How much time do you have?
Estimate how long a task will last – and then check to see if you were right	Are you on track?
Break work / homework down into short time segments	What you need to do comes before what you *want* to do
	Honestly, how long will it really take?
Other strategies:	**Your own idea(s):**

WEEKLY PLANNER

Week: [add date]	Monday	Tuesday	Wednesday	Thursday	Friday
Before school					
Period 1					
Period 2					
Period 3					
Period 4					
Period 5					
Period 6					
After school					

TASKS TO BE ACCOMPLISHED THIS WEEK

Tasks to be accomplished this week	Time allowance	Actual time taken
1.		
2.		
3.		

NIGHTLY HOMEWORK PLANNER

Task: detail of homework activity	Time estimation	Actual time taken	Complete / not complete?

Term planner example:

Monday	Tuesday	Wednesday	Thursday	Friday	Saturday	Sunday
		Nov. 25th	26th	27th	28th	29th
30th	Dec. 1st	2nd	3rd	4th	5th	6th
7th	8th	9th	10th	11th	XMAS BREAK	XMAS BREAK

PROJECT SHEET / PLANNER

Project set date:	Project due date:
Project title:	
Sub topic 1:	To be completed by:
Sub topic 2:	To be completed by:
Sub topic 3:	To be completed by:

The following example is for an internal end of topic test where the teacher sets it one week in advance.

REVISION PLAN

Subject:	Test focus:
6 days before the test	I will cover:
5 days before the test	I will cover:
4 days before the test	I will cover:
3 days before the test	I will cover:
2 days before the test	I will cover:
1 day before the test	Review all revision and look at practice questions
Test reflections:	What went well? What could I improve?

FOR THOSE PUPILS WHO NEED ADDITIONAL, MORE FOCUSED SUPPORT WITHIN THE CLASSROOM

- Work with the pupil to prioritise tasks.

- Provide them with a 'to do' list on their desk to work through in a set time – use timers to show the passage of time.

- Break tasks into smaller sections each with a set time limit to complete them – provide a visual / checklist where possible.

- Appoint a 'time management buddy' who can help them get to class on time / keep them on track.

- Check in with them on a personal level regularly so that they are accountable.

- Celebrate achievements and successes.

- Draw their attention to the passage of time through the visual use of clocks and timers.

CHAPTER 14

Working Memory

EF skill	Explanation	Classroom impact
Working memory	The ability to hold something in mind while you perform complex tasks. It includes the ability to use past experiences to apply now or in the future Working memory consists of visual (or non-verbal) recall and verbal (or language-based) recall	• Difficulty keeping track of possessions • Difficulty remembering what you have to do • Not learning from past experiences • Difficulty following classroom instruction • Finding it hard to hold maths problems / essay structures etc. in mind to successfully complete them

What is working memory?

Working memory is one of the first EF skills to begin to develop, starting in infancy. It is a type of short-term memory (as opposed to long-term memory, which is much more permanent, where we store and consolidate facts and memories), which allows us to store information for a short period of time and to use key pieces of that information and do something with it or add to it. Usually, we have a working memory capacity of being able to remember about seven items.

We use our working memory whenever holding or processing two or more pieces of information in our heads. This includes, for example:

- The ability to hold in mind, piece together and make sense of the beginning of a passage as we read to the end of it.

- The ability to remember a whole conversation and be able to respond to it, by being able to recall from the beginning to the last part of what someone says, and then to make sense of it.

- Being able to hold multistep instructions in mind.

- The ability to recall information from the long-term memory and link it with new information.

- Being able to multitask by holding the tasks in mind, e.g., remembering the need to copy homework assignments from the board, pack up, and remembering where to go next.

- When solving a mental arithmetic calculation.

Working memory can be improved!

According to Baddeley (1996), 'Working memory consists of a central executive, a phonological loop [the processing of auditory information] and a visuo-spatial sketchpad [the processing of visual and spatial information]' (p.5), with the central executive controlling attention and coordinating both the phonological loop and visuo-spatial sketchpad. Not only does this tell us that working memory is a core EF skill that is housed in the prefrontal cortex of the brain, but it also suggests that information that is both verbally and visually presented should be more memorable because it engages all facets of working memory. As teachers, it is clear that we should try to teach both verbally *and* visually wherever possible.

And we have different **types** of memory: information we hold temporarily in our short-term memory, our active working memory and long-term memory. Often analogies of our memory are likened to computers, with the short-term memory being the information displayed on the screen in front of you and not available to you once you close the page; our long-term memory is often likened to the hard drive that holds on to information until it is deleted; and our working memory is said to be the equivalent of the RAM that processes the new information.

The brain has an amazing capacity to assess and process new information and to respond to important stuff by reordering it or sorting it for possible retention; it also discards about 99 per cent of the information it receives because it does not need to be retained. Working memory allows us to take in new information, do something with it and hold it in mind for a short time, while the brain assimilates whether it needs to be stored or not. The long-term memory changes slowly as new information is embedded in it.

Difficulties with working memory can be exacerbated if a pupil is prone to distractibility and impulsive decision making. This can lead to difficulties forgetting work and forgetting instructions, and it can mean that these pupils misplace things more easily and are more forgetful than their peers. However, everyone can struggle with focus and application to some extent if they do not find the task they are doing very interesting. Added to this is what was discovered by Hermann Ebbinghaus (1885 [1962]) in his Forgetting Curve model. Ebbinghaus was a German psychologist who explored memory and the ability to forget. Among other fascinating memory facts he found that humans find it hard to retain more than 10 per cent of their learning over a 30-day period – which means pupils are at risk of forgetting a whopping 90 per cent of what they have been taught if information is presented to them just once without any opportunities for review(s)! Therefore, teachers need to try to build in as many opportunities as possible for review and repetition, spanned over days and weeks, to try to help it to stick and embed in students' long-term memory. Making links with prior learning also helps to make new knowledge more meaningful and assists the memory process.

It is interesting to explore with students how they remember information best – whether it is from what they see, what they do, what they hear, when they work collaboratively or what they discuss. The use of imagination is also a powerful memory tool, as is the ability to create mental images, and being able to link memories to help them embed. Some pupils may never have considered these different ways of recalling information, but if it can be made an ongoing topic of discussion within the classroom, it will help them to assess and reassess how information is 'sticking' in their minds, and whether they have a way that works particularly well for them.

What you might see in a child who has a poor working memory

- They forget to bring necessary kit into school, to take necessary kit home, and do not have the correct materials needed for class / home.

- They forget to record homework properly, miss deadlines and do not hand in homework on time.

- They forget due dates for longer-term projects or tests, and miss deadlines.

- They lose their train of thought.

- They have difficulty following instructions, particularly if there are multiple steps.

- They lose things or forget where they have been left.

The developmental stages of working memory

The developmental stages that you might expect to see for working memory look something like this:

- Nursery-aged children (typically 2–4) can hold things in mind and remember them for a short period of time, often with adult supervision. We might expect them to be able to remember immediate instructions.

- As children get older, they are able to retain information for longer periods of time and with less supervision and less immediacy to perform a required task.

- Children aged approximately 5–8 begin to be able to hold more than one instruction in mind, building this skill, as well as being able to hold on to the instruction for longer.

- Children typically aged 8–11 can begin to remember delayed tasks without being reminded – so, for example, they can remember they need to complete homework without being prompted, and can begin to pack bags for school independently (especially when they are not expected to take multiple text and exercise books to and from school). They can retain some steps or instructions long enough to complete them.

- Children aged 11–16 are expected to be able to move from teacher to teacher and remember what their timetable is without constant reminders. They can also pack their bags for school and remember to complete and hand in their homework at the correct time. They can retain several steps / sets of instructions to complete class-based tasks.

The following checklist will help teachers gauge how well they support working memory in the classroom.

TEACHER SELF-REVIEW CHECKLIST: WORKING MEMORY

I support students' working memory by:	Yes	No
Giving an overview of my lesson at the beginning		
Adapting my teaching to reduce demands on those I know have working memory difficulties		
Making clear links with previous learning to make it more meaningful		
Breaking tasks down into smaller, achievable tasks		
Displaying key information on the board		
Repeating instructions and recording them visually to be checked off when done		
My own ideas...		

Ways you can model and support students to develop their own working memory (and help to transfer information from working memory to long-term memory)

- Use written reminders – lists, Post-it® notes, calendars etc.

- Model the use and importance of 'to do' lists – how to make a 'to do' list and how to maintain and manage it by crossing off completed items and adding new ones to the list when they occur. You can also model and promote how to prioritise items on the list in terms of their importance.

- Use coloured markers to highlight instructions (use different colours to signal different things, such as green for the most important, red for things you might be likely to forget). Highlight important information.

- The process of recalling or recognising information stored in our memory is known as retrieval. Model putting things away in the correct place when you have finished using them and draw attention to the fact you are doing this so you can recall where to locate them next time.

- Write and say instructions to engage the visual and verbal aspects of memory.

- Repeat and recap information.

- Making teaching multisensory will help embed the information and make it more memorable.

- Creating rhymes, mnemonics and chants applicable to the subject being taught will aid recall.

- Flashcards and putting information to music or to actions helps make it multisensory, which all helps to embed information.

- Chunk the information you are giving, to break it up into more manageable segments.

- Where possible and relevant, consider making lessons less wordy and more interactive, to help embed information.

- Give pupils prior warning about homework tasks at the start of lessons and not at the end, so there is time for pupils to assimilate what they need to do and to understand it – especially in the context of the lesson that is being taught.

- Provide copies of multiplication charts, spelling lists etc.

- Provide copies of notes.

Classroom ideas for teachers to help with working memory

- Teach pupils to get into the habit of highlighting important information.

- Try to make eye contact with pupils before telling them something you want them to remember.

- Make sure there are minimal distractions when delivering important information that you want pupils to remember – and model to them that distractions do just that – distract them!

- If you are not sure whether a particular pupil who you know has challenges in this area has really heard / listened to you, (discreetly and sympathetically) ask them to paraphrase what you have said, back to you.

- Encourage pupils to use written reminders – lists, Post-it® notes, calendars etc.

- Encourage pupils to use technological solutions to aid working memory by setting reminders of specific events etc. (apps, smartphones, digital calendars). Encourage those pupils who need it to set reminders with time and sound cues on their smartphones.

- Encourage pupils to 'teach you' / 'teach a partner' (e.g., get them to practise explaining a skill or activity). This helps them to remember all the steps needed to complete the task.

- Work on visualisation skills (encourage pupils to try to create a visual picture in their head of what they have just heard / want to remember). Visual images can help to strengthen memory muscle for a piece of information – encourage pupils to develop meaningful mental images.

- Emphasise the importance of keeping a 'homework diary' to record work set and due dates. Encourage pupils to enter tasks into a schedule and consider the effect of writing the due date in a different colour and orientation (e.g., vertical instead of horizontal), so that it stands out as being something different to tasks that are set.

- Practise active reading strategies (taking notes, using sticky notes, asking questions as they are reading etc.).

- Promote the use of coloured markers to signal different things, such as green for the most important, red for things the student might be likely to forget.

- Encourage pupils to get into the habit of putting things away in the correct place when they have finished using them, so that they know where to locate them next time.

- Brain training activities can significantly improve concentration skills. If there is 'free time' in class (in form time, at the end of term etc.), consider getting pupils to do the following activities: Sudoku, crossword puzzles, chess, jigsaw puzzles, word searches, Scrabble, Pairs, Kim's Game, I Spy, spot the difference, Crazy Eights, Uno, Go Fish etc.

The importance of involving pupils in preview and review strategies

The preview / review concept can be used to develop and promote pupils' self-advocacy.

- Asking pupils to engage with course materials to initiate their own topic or lesson preview will encourage them to read ahead and get an overview of what will be covered in the topic or next lesson. This helps to make learning more meaningful because the pupils have actively engaged in it. These kinds of activities will help to develop pupils' working memory as well as helping to embed their learning in their long-term memory.

- When preparing for a test, encouraging pupils to review the topic in its entirety will help to give them an overview of it before they start breaking the task down and revising the finer details. Creating an overview sheet will help to refresh their memory and make the detailed learning more meaningful by anchoring it within context.

- This can be taken a stage further and a simple 'Test preview and review' sheet could be used to encourage self-reflection. Pupils could be asked to predict how they think they might fare in an upcoming test, based on their perception of their subject knowledge and how well they believe they applied themselves to their learning. After the test they could reflect on how they actually did. This kind of exercise becomes a powerful tool if the information is then used as a comparison for pupils to self-reflect and analyse whether there is a difference in their self-awareness and their outcomes. This provides something tangible to refer back to when preparing for the next test and trying to learn from previous experiences.

- This concept of preview and review can also be adopted in class to make learning as memorable and meaningful as possible. Building routines into lessons where the teacher reviews (briefly) what was covered in the previous lesson, and previews what will be being covered in the upcoming lesson, will help to contextualise new knowledge and link it to prior learning. When new learning can be stacked on top of pre-existing understanding, it has a much greater chance of sticking. This approach complements Ebbinghaus's Forgetting Curve model (1885 [1962]), which highlights the need for multiple opportunities for review in order to maximise pupils' ability to retain information.

Resources

WORKING MEMORY CHECKLIST

Tip: When thinking how to improve and support working memory, the key is to reduce the distractions so that you have more mental capacity to focus. Working memory can be supported by listing the important tasks being held in mind, and using colours and highlighting to make important tasks and deadlines stand out.

I can support my working memory by:	Yes	No
Previewing what we are going to be learning in class by reading ahead		
Reviewing what I have learned by going back over the lesson / learning		
Regularly reviewing my planner / homework record and having a good understanding of what I need to do each day / week		
Planning my work before starting		
Other ideas...		

FOR THOSE PUPILS WHO NEED ADDITIONAL, MORE FOCUSED SUPPORT WITHIN THE CLASSROOM

- For those who need extra scaffolding, encourage them to write themselves more explicit / detailed reminders about tasks that need to be done, to trigger their memory more effectively, e.g., by encouraging them to write, and how to make notes for multistep directions.

- Provide specific alerts when essential material or instructions are being presented.

- You may need to provide additional processing time or time to rehearse the information.

- New information and instructions may need to be kept brief and to the point or repeated.

- Provide a hard copy of essential information such as facts, main ideas or a list of steps for problem solving or an assignment.

- Providing an outline or a set of notes at the start of class can alleviate working memory demands and allow the pupil to listen actively rather than trying to listen, hold information and write it down in real time.

- Provide breaks of only 1 or 2 minutes.

- Provide preferential seating to allow for increased supervision.

- Use cues to help the pupil to focus on the correct bit of information or word.

CHAPTER 15

Metacognition

EF skill	Explanation	Classroom impact
Metacognition	The ability to be self-aware of your skills as a learner and how you respond to events – taking a bird's eye look at yourself	• Difficulty with understanding your own learning behaviour and your own learning journey • Difficulty planning, evaluating and regulating your thoughts • Your own understanding of yourself – 'I have difficulty learning times tables/spellings' etc.

What is metacognition?

Metacognition involves understanding how you problem solve and decide what is called for in a given situation by asking yourself 'How am I doing?', and afterwards being able to evaluate how you fared and to subsequently use that knowledge to decide how to do things in the future. This links to Dweck's growth mindset (see Chapter 3), which promotes the development of cognitive flexibility and willingness to learn from setbacks, and an understanding that practice (rather than inherent skills) makes perfect.

Metacognitive awareness involves:

- Being able to make adjustments. If Plan A doesn't work, being prepared to have a Plan B and to be able to evaluate performance by thinking through the consequences and considering 'if I do this, then what will happen next?' This is linked to the EF skill of 'flexibility' (see Chapter 7).

- An ability to be able to see what the impact of ourselves and our own behaviour might have on others.

- The ability to take a bird's eye view of ourself by being able to stand back and observe ourself from the outside.

Young children tend to be good at self-advocacy – they live in the present and can be vocal in expressing their immediate needs and wants. However, they tend to do this in the absence of an awareness beyond themselves. They often do not consider the consequences of their desires, and usually fail to take into consideration the responses and reactions of those around them. This ability to put themselves first and assert their needs reduces as they grow older and become more socially aware. They learn to exert more self-control and become more concerned about what the outside world thinks of them.

Despite this natural sense of progression, many pupils need to be taught what metacognition truly means and how to be metacognitive.

What you might see in a child who has poor metacognitive awareness

- They have difficulty accurately evaluating skills (e.g., expecting to do well in tests, despite poor past performance / preparation).

- They do not respond to and learn from feedback.

- They are unable to identify appropriate study strategies.

- They do not plan or organise a written piece of work.

- They are able to memorise facts but miss the bigger context (they do better on multiple choice tests than essay questions).

- They have difficulty with abstract understanding.

- They do not know what to study.

- They have difficulty understanding the material.

- They do a poor job and get into trouble for it.

- They do not proofread and check their work.

The following checklist will help teachers gauge how well they support metacognition in the classroom.

TEACHER SELF-REVIEW CHECKLIST: METACOGNITION

I support students' metacognition and self-reflection by:	Yes	No
Employing the 'assess, plan, do, review' model to my teaching		
Asking students to think about what strategies worked best / worst for them in a task		
Modelling metacognitive talk – what do I know about this topic already? / what would I like to know? etc.		
Providing meaningful feedback		
Promoting resilience and perseverance		
Modelling the process of planning, monitoring and evaluating performance in a task		
Encouraging inquisitiveness and questioning		
My own ideas...		

At the beginning of the day, preview what you hope to achieve and how, and at the end of the day, review it and reflect on what worked well and what didn't, so that your professional practice is constantly developing and improving.

Ways you can model and support students to develop their own metacognition

- Mastering metacognition does not just apply to pupils. As teachers we need to be self-aware and able to self-reflect – especially if we, in turn, are trying to teach these self-appraisal skills to pupils.

- Students are likely to be more relaxed and engaged in lessons where there is an open atmosphere, where metacognitive skills are modelled and there is a sense of learning together. Mistakes and differences in approach need to become accepted as part of the learning process rather than seen as failures or something to be embarrassed about. This is particularly true for teenagers who may find the process of self-reflection difficult if it is not in line with the opinions of their peers. Developing a culture of self-analysis about academic effort and application will help in starting to create a higher level of metacognitive awareness in pupils, which will eventually have wider-reaching benefits for them.

- Encouraging pupils to take risks and to think outside the box, without worrying about how friends might judge them, is cognitive flexibility! It requires them to step outside their comfort zone and to be open-minded to listening to the advice of others (and not just their friends). Pupils should be encouraged to consider if the best scenario is not working out, what might be the next best scenario / decision that they can make. These are skills they can then employ in other fields of their lives as they become more familiar with the concept of self-reflection.

- If you can regularly model some carefully chosen self-reflective behaviour to the students, for those who have yet to understand and develop a sense of metacognitive awareness, it will give them concrete examples of what it looks like and help them to learn from example.

  - Model self-reflection and the skill of self-talk to pupils. When you do this, label it and name what you are doing so that those who have not yet developed their internal voice can begin to understand what it is and how to use it.

- Provide meaningful praise (for the effort and approach rather than the outcome) as well as feedback and constructive ways to improve, so that pupils make the correlation that process is more important than results. Your aim is that pupils will learn to understand that feedback from you will always be helpful even if it is constructive criticism, and that it is okay to receive this kind of feedback because it is all geared towards helping them to improve, rather than marking them for what they do and do not know, which may well correlate with success and failure.

- Recap the last lesson at the beginning of the next, and also give a preview / insight of the next lesson at the end of the current one to enable pupils to predict ahead and know what to expect. This can help them develop autonomy and ownership over their learning and develop their self-awareness as a learner.

Classroom ideas for teachers to help with metacognition difficulties

- As teachers, we cannot truly motivate a student to succeed – that has to be self-directed! While we can offer external incentives / rewards and punishments to get them to conform, we should instead be encouraging students to be driven by their own internal drive. We can begin to do this by asking them to think about what kinds of things motivate them and trying to help them create 'hooks' linked to their personal motivation factors that will engage them in their learning and allow them to become self-motivated.

- Teachers can begin to foster metacognitive awareness by:

  - Demonstrating and reinforcing what success criteria looks like

  - Providing constructive feedback to pupils, explaining how they can learn from it and improve for next time

  - Checking in with pupils to ensure that they are still on track

  - Creating time within lessons to encourage students to reflect on their performance and evaluate how to improve

- Encouraging revising and proofreading of completed pieces of work – this also promotes self-analysis

- Providing specific praise for task performance, by recognising strategies that the pupil uses, e.g., performance on schoolwork, interactions with friends etc. – 'you're good at understanding your friends' feelings'

- Teaching students how to use the self-talk you use when you want to master or succeed in something – 'I'm going to work at this problem until I understand how it works / develops / etc.'

- Also teaching them how to engage in self-praise, where their internal voice congratulates them on successes – 'I persevered with my algebra homework; I didn't stop or give up until I finished it'

- Encouraging pupils to be seeking feedback (from others, e.g., you as their teacher) as a way to improve performance

- Considering getting into the habit of asking pupils to include a short self-evaluation at the end of each piece of work

- Starting working with pupils to explore how they learn

- Asking pupils to self-assess areas that they know they could improve on – proofreading their work or checking the accuracy of recording their maths calculations. If you encourage a special focus on these areas and see if pupils can identify their own errors by proofreading and reviewing what they have done, they can then create their own self-assessment sheet to help them remember what to pay special attention to when they review their work.

Resources

Here are some worksheets and checklists for pupils to complete.

WORKSHEET: MANAGING METACOGNITION

When working through this worksheet if you feel you are good at the skill identified, tick the 'not a problem' box. If, however, it is an area you feel you need to tackle, record your thoughts (maybe why you find it tricky / how you might try to practice improvement) in the 'notes' section.

Item	Not a problem	Notes
I follow instructions and complete all the steps for pieces of work to make sure I have the opportunity to do well		
I proofread my work for careless mistakes		
I know what to study		
I know how to study		
I understand the material of the subject		
I avoid doing a poor job and getting into trouble for it		

Here are some self-help strategies for pupils.

Tips	Self-talk
Ask teachers for revision sheets for tests	What's the big picture?
Create your own study packs for tests by pulling together all important material, amalgamating and condensing your notes	How are you doing?
Create self-monitoring checklists (e.g., a proofreading checklist)	What worked for you before?

Ask yourself four self-monitoring questions: What is my problem? What is my plan? Am I following my plan? How did I do?	What didn't work?
	What do you need or want for a grade?
Tips	**Self-talk**
	Have you studied enough to get it?
Other strategies:	**Your own idea(s):**

PROOFREADING CHECKLIST

- Do all sentences begin with a capital letter?

- Have all proper nouns got capital letters?

- Are all sentences complete sentences?

- Did I use appropriate paragraphs, with one key idea per paragraph?

- Do all sentences have ending punctuation? (. ! ?)

- Did I use commas and quotation marks correctly?

- Did I spell every word correctly?

THREE-COLOUR HIGHLIGHTING

- Main points (often the first or last paragraph in a section or the first sentence in a paragraph).

- Supporting details (elaborating on the main points, provides evidence or proof to support assertions or opinions).

- Terms (key vocabulary or concepts).

K-W-L TECHNIQUE

- K = Background knowledge

- W = What you would like to know about the topic

- L = Learned (read the material and note what you have learned)

Know	Want to learn	Learned

WORKSHEET: PROBLEM SOLVING

1. Identify the problem

    . . . .

    . . . .

2. List the possible solutions to resolve the problem

    . . . .

    . . . .

3. Rank them in terms of feasibility / likelihood of success

    . . . .

    . . . .

4. Try the best ranked solution

    . . . .

    . . . .

5. Did it work? If not, why not?

    . . . .

    . . . .

6. Try the second most feasible solution, etc.

    . . . .

    . . . .

7. How can I avoid this problem in the future?

    . . . .

    . . . .

WORKSHEET: HOW YOU SEE YOURSELF AND HOW OTHERS SEE YOU

How I see myself:

. . . .

. . . .

How others might see me:

. . . .

. . . .

What are the main differences?

. . . .

. . . .

Would I change anything?

. . . .

. . . .

My positive relationships are with:

. . . .

. . . .

Why? / How?

. . . .

. . . .

My trickier relationships are with:

. . . .

. . . .

Why? / How?

. . . .

. . . .

WORKSHEET: SELF-REFLECTION

1. Describe yourself: good and bad parts

   . . . .

   . . . .

2. Describe how you think others see you

. . . .

. . . .

3. How do they compare?

. . . .

. . . .

4. How do you want to see yourself?

. . . .

. . . .

This can be developed and taken further by encouraging the pupil to make a list of the EF skills that they need to work on and why – how it interferes with their life, what sense of difficulty / chaos it creates, what they can do to get on top of it so that they are in better control, who they can ask for assistance etc.

TASK MINDSET CHECKER

1. What is your mindset at the beginning of the task? E.g.

   - I'm okay doing it.

   - I really don't want to do it.

   - Keen to get it done quickly.

   - I will do it well even if it takes time.

   . . . .

   . . . .

2. What is affecting your mindset? E.g.

- I like this subject and I'm looking forward to it.

- I dislike this subject and I'm not looking forward to it.

- I have something I'd rather be doing.

- I'm okay prioritising this because I know I need to do it.

....

....

3. How long do you estimate it will take?

....

....

4. Do you need to break it down into chunks, or can you do it in one sitting?

....

....

NOW COMPLETE THE TASK

1. Did your mindset remain constant or change? If so, what affected the change?

....

....

2. Was your time estimate accurate? If not, why?

....

....

3. Did you achieve what you wanted to?

....

....

4. What strategies did you use?

....

....

5. How do you feel now?

....

....

6. What have you learned that might help you to approach a similar task in the future?

....

....

7. Did you learn anything about yourself?

....

....

8. Can you transfer any of the skills you used for this task to the next piece of work you have to do, to make it easier for you?

....

....

WORKSHEET: DEVELOPING SELF-AWARENESS

I am good at...

....

. . . .

I find it difficult to...

. . . .

. . . .

When I find something difficult I...

. . . .

. . . .

My best way of learning is...

. . . .

. . . .

I could become even better by...

. . . .

. . . .

WORKSHEET: EXAM SELF-REFLECTION, BEFORE THE EXAM

1. I started preparing for this exam: (circle which one applies)

   - Last night

   - About a week ago

   - About a month ago

   - All term / year (I have been keeping on top of my learning and studying)

2. My revision strategies have been: (fill in how you have prepared for this exam)

   . . . .

   . . . .

3. I feel: (circle which one applies)

- Unprepared

- I wish I had done a bit more

- Well prepared

4. What (if anything) I would do differently next time:

. . . .

. . . .

WORKSHEET: EXAM SELF-REFLECTION, AFTER THE EXAM

1. I feel I did: (circle which one applies)

- Not well

- Not sure

- Well

- Very well

2. Why have you given the answer you did to this question? Circle which of the following applies:

- I was generally unprepared

- There were some areas / topics I needed to know a bit more about

- I was quite well prepared – but I wish I had done more work on: (fill in below)

  - a.

  - b.

  - c.

  - etc.

- I feel very confident about my performance

3. What (if anything) I would do differently next time:

. . . .

. . . .

FOR THOSE PUPILS WHO NEED ADDITIONAL, MORE FOCUSED SUPPORT WITHIN THE CLASSROOM

Those pupils who have particular difficulties with the skill of impulse control may find it harder to engage their metacognitive thinking skills, that is, to stand back and see themselves, and to assess what is or is not working for them, and what to do about it. These pupils, more than others, may also need assistance, for example, in:

- Trying to spot changes of behaviour in others – so if a teacher's tone of voice changes, or their manner and body language changes, some pupils will need explicit guidance to recognise this by developing better listening and observational skills, as well as the ability to respond appropriately, and then to stand back afterwards and to self-reflect what might have caused that tonal change.

- Self-reflection – initially they may need to take a step back, pause and consider what someone important in their lives (typically it tends to be a family member) would advise them to do in this situation. This is because they have not yet developed their internal voice and are still reliant on external motivators. By encouraging them to think what someone else would advise them to do, you are moving them closer to eventually being able to consider what *they* might do in that situation.

PART 3

AWARENESS AND HOME ENVIRONMENT

The following chapter will explain the benefits of liaising with the home environment (parents etc.) to gain their support, so that they understand EF skills and their importance. It will also provide a series of downloadable resources that explain EF skills. These will encourage the adults in the home environment to support the work that teachers are doing, so that the child is supported both at home and at school, for optimal EF development.

The resources are found wherever you see the symbol 🔁 and can be downloaded from https://digitalhub.jkp.com/redeem using the code UNPVSWJ.

CHAPTER 16

How Parents Can Help to Support and Hone Executive Function Skills

Teachers cannot influence parenting style or homelife values, but if you have the opportunity to get parents (and caregivers) on board with the ethos of honing good EF skills, then without doubt this will only be to the benefit of the pupils you teach, because it will raise awareness with parents who can help to reinforce the skills that you are addressing in the classroom.

Basic things that complement EF skills that parents can promote at home are good sleep, good hygiene, good nutrition and good exercise habits, as we know these all help a student to function more efficiently, both at school and in their home lives.

In terms of how parents might specifically support each of the EF skills, a series of guides for parents has been produced.

Guides for parents

The following guides have been created to complement school-based foci. They are designed to be adapted if you wish, and to be sent to parents each time you address a new EF skill. I recommend that you send the relevant guide to parents as you introduce a new EF skill to the pupils, rather than all in one go. I also suggest that you send a letter / email to parents in advance, to explain what you are doing, and why.

The first guide explains what EF skills are and sows the seed for the ways parents can begin to support EF skills at home. The remaining guides each focus on a different EF skill.

Guide 1: What are executive function (EF) skills?

Our EF skills help us to regulate our behaviour, make and achieve goals, and balance demands and desires, wants, needs and 'have to' haves.

Everyone has strengths and weaknesses. The more someone knows about their own EF skills profile, the more they can take advantage of their natural strengths, while developing a plan to strengthen their weaker skills.

What are the individual EF skills?

- Response inhibition
- Emotional control
- Flexibility
- Task initiation
- Sustained attention
- Goal-directed persistence
- Planning and prioritisation
- Organisation
- Time management
- Working memory
- Metacognition

EF definitions

EF skill	Definition	Examples
Response inhibition	Self-restraint, the capacity to think before you act, the ability to resist the urge to say or do something, allowing you time to evaluate the situation and how your behaviour may have an impact	• Acting before you think • Not thinking about the consequences • Blurting out answers/thoughts and not being able to wait until asked
Emotional control	The ability to regulate your emotions The ability to conduct healthy personal and school-based relationships	• Getting easily frustrated • Getting stressed • Getting easily upset • Arguing back with teacher / pupils • Finding it hard to control exuberance in class / with peers
Flexibility	The ability to be adaptable and to be willing to change plans and direction, where needed	• Finding it hard to 'go with the flow' • Finding it hard when plans change • Getting upset if things don't go according to plan • Difficulty switching easily between tasks / moving between lesson topics – wanting to finish a previous task and finding it hard to move on
Task initiation	The ability to start tasks without putting them off	• Finding it hard to stop doing something that interests you in order to prioritise work (playing online games, social media etc.) • Finding it hard to get straight on with tasks set by the teacher – requiring input to get started or using strategies (sharpening pencils, going to the loo, filling a water bottle) to put off starting

EF skill	Definition	Examples
Sustained attention	The ability to focus and pay attention, even if the task is not very engaging	• Difficulty following through and being able to complete a task without supervision, or external pressure to complete it • Starting something and not finishing it • In class finding it hard to work for the required period without distraction
Goal-directed persistence	The ability to meet targets and goals, by sticking at it until finished	• Difficulty with persisting at something • Giving up on things • Finding it hard to complete a project / persist with revision
Planning and prioritisation	The ability to plan how to achieve a desired goal / outcome and to prioritise the steps needed to achieve it	• Difficulty knowing how / where to start on a task • Difficulty in having an idea of the steps you need to go through to complete a project • Not knowing how to plan an essay
Organisation	The ability to have a well-ordered mind and to be neat, tidy and methodical with possessions and workspaces	• Messy, chaotic school bag • Disorganised notes • Difficulty finding things
Time management	The ability to understand the passage of time and an awareness of how long something will take Being aware of submission dates and deadlines	• Lack of punctuality, e.g., getting to lessons on time • Difficulty finishing schoolwork in a timely manner • Difficulty maintaining routines and deadlines • Difficulty working out how long something will take • Missing dates and deadlines

Working memory	The ability to hold something in mind while you perform complex tasks; this includes the ability to use past experiences to apply now or in the future Working memory consists of visual (or non-verbal) recall and verbal (or language-based) recall	• Difficulty keeping track of possessions • Difficulty remembering what you have to do • Not learning from past experiences • Difficulty following classroom instructions • Finding it hard to hold maths problems / essay structures etc. in mind to successfully complete them
Metacognition	The ability to be self-aware: of your skills as a learner and how you respond to events – taking a bird's eye look at yourself	• Difficulty with understanding your own learning behaviour and your own learning journey • Difficulty planning, evaluating and regulating your thoughts • Your own understanding of yourself – 'I have difficulty learning times tables / spellings' etc.

Key facts

- Our EF skills continue to develop into our twenties.

- It is perfectly normal to be better at some EF skills than others. It becomes challenging when some / all of these skills are sufficiently tricky for an individual to manage so that they lead to academic or social and emotional challenges.

Guide 2: Helping your child to understand their executive function (EF) profile

There are two dimensions of EF skills – thinking and doing. The frontal lobes of the brain (prefrontal cortex) are the 'executives in charge' and can be compared to the leaders or supervisors of organisations. Without good leadership, the organisation becomes unstructured and inefficient.

Knowing which EF skills belong to which group of skills will help you to know whether your child needs help with thinking differently or behaving differently:

EF skills involving thinking (cognition)	EF skills involving doing (behaviour)
Planning and prioritisation	Response inhibition
Organisation	Emotional control
Time management	Flexibility
Working memory	Task initiation
Metacognition	Sustained attention
	Goal-directed persistence

Source: Based on Guare, Dawson and Guare (2013, p.19)

How do EF skills involving thinking affect learning?	How do EF skills involving behaviour affect learning?
Making plans	Waiting to speak until we are called upon
Meaningfully including past knowledge in discussions / work	Changing our minds and making mid-course corrections while thinking, reading and writing
Evaluating ideas and reflecting on work	Engaging in group dynamics
Keeping track of more than one thing at once	Asking for help or seeking more information when we need it
Keeping track of time and finishing work on time	

General strategies

- Encourage your child to break down their work into smaller sections to make it more manageable.

- Promote the use of time organisers, watches with alarms, alerts etc. to remind them when to do something.

- Provide visual timetables for the school week (lessons, days homework is set and due dates, if this information is available to you) that you might put somewhere visible (e.g., in the kitchen), and get them to review it and refer to it several times a day.

- Encourage your child to seek written directions along with oral instructions if they need to – an email to a teacher if uncertain etc.

- Help your child to be aware of and plan for transition times and shifts in activities during the day, so that they are more prepared for this as they progress through the day.

Managing time

- Encourage your child to create checklists / 'to do' lists, and to estimate how long each task will take. Getting them to review afterwards how long a task took is also a helpful way to develop an understanding of time.

- Encourage them to break projects into smaller sections and assign a time frame for completing each part.

- Use calendars displayed in a communal space, such as the kitchen, to help your child keep track of deadlines for longer-term projects, tasks and activities. If it is in a shared space, you can use it to check in with your child, to monitor their progress in a non-intrusive way.

Managing space and equipment

- Encourage your child to keep a clutter-free workspace.

- Schedule a weekly time for them to clean and organise their workspace.

Managing work

- Encourage your child to keep checklists about work set, due dates, reading all directions before attempting to start a task etc.

- Encourage them to troubleshoot problems, so that they are taking more control of their anxieties.

Guide 3: Response inhibition

Response inhibition is the capacity to think before you act. While it is important to remember that EF skills are 'interactive', that is, they work together and depend on each other, some believe that working on improving response inhibition will also result in improvement of the other EF skills in children.

Behavioural inhibition has been described as occurring in three versions:

- The ability to stop or inhibit a response before it begins.
- The ability to stop or inhibit a response that has already begun.
- The ability to pause, block or delay a reaction or response to a situation until it is more appropriate to do so.

One example of response inhibition is: a child begins to get lost in a lesson, and instead of trying to remain calm and persevering to see if they get back on track, they get into an anxious state and fail to block the anxiety from taking over. Another example is losing focus and allowing attention to wander and drift.

The following worksheet can be adapted to a situation that regularly triggers a poor response inhibition reaction.

WORKSHEET: FLEXIBILITY / PROBLEM SOLVING

1. Identify the problem
2. Brainstorm solutions
3. Ask your child to choose the solutions that they prefer
4. Discuss Plan A, and if that does not work, what is Plan B?
5. Make a visual reminder

Here is a worked example.

What is the problem?
E.g., *I get panicky if I feel I do not understand a lesson, and I lose concentration.*

How might I begin to solve the problem?
- *Let the teacher know I've got a bit lost, and wait for them to help me.*
- *Take deep breaths to try to calm myself down, so I can stay in the lesson and hopefully refocus.*
- My own ideas...[whatever strategies work for your child / family]

What are the possible solutions?

List the priorities of Plan A, B, C

Start with Plan A, e.g.,

- *I know I can ask the teacher to help.*

If that didn't work, move on to Plan B, e.g.,

- *I know I can ask a classmate to help me.*

My own ideas...

Self-reflect: What went well?

What might I do differently next time?

Guide 4: Emotional control

Emotional control is the capacity to regulate emotional responses.

What you might see in your child if they have poor emotional control

- They have a tendency to react quickly or spontaneously.

- They have difficulty receiving negative feedback.

- They show an emotional response that is stronger than their peers exhibit, or that is greater than expected.

- They find it difficult to maintain perspective and see the bigger picture.

- They find it hard to see the other person's perspective.

- They find it hard to move on and forget about something.

How to help with emotional control difficulties

- Encourage your child to 'breathe through' the emotional surge.

- Practise relaxation techniques with your child.

- Anticipate and visualise some of the more positive emotions they will feel when the moment of emotional dysregulation passes – this will help the moment to pass more quickly.

- Being aware of their emotional responses and how to manage them will help your child to:

  - Take a step back and pause before reacting.

  - Walk away from the situation so as not to inflame it further.

  - Allow a cooling off time.

  - See the bigger picture, as well as promoting seeing things from someone else's perspective.

Here are some self-help strategies for you to encourage your child to do.

Tips	Self-talk
Be aware of your unique temptations and make a plan to avoid them	First work, then play
Ask yourself, 'Good choice or bad choice?'	Learn from your mistakes
Practise waiting (e.g., add a little more time or work before giving yourself the reward)	Stop and think
Other strategies:	**Your own idea(s):**
Tips	**Self-talk**
Label the feeling and let it go	Take 10 seconds
When you can, walk away from the upsetting situation, get a hold of yourself, and come back	Take deep breaths
Look into learning meditation techniques	This, too, shall pass

Pat yourself on the back when you stay cool	Big deal or little deal?
Other strategies:	**Your own idea(s):**

Guide 5: Flexibility

Flexibility is the ability to adapt and revise plans when conditions change; for example, when obstacles and setbacks arise, when new information becomes available, and when mistakes occur.

You have flexibility if you 'go with the flow' and do not get thrown by last-minute changes.

Exercising flexibility means that instead of being disappointed or upset when changes occur you start thinking about how you can solve the problem and find ways around it.

What you might see in your child if they have poor flexibility

- They struggle with open-ended tasks or when there are several different approaches to choose from.

- They go down one route (e.g., to complete a piece of work), and if it's not working well, they find it really difficult to stop, adapt and take a different approach.

- 'White paper syndrome' – they find it really hard to generate ideas to get going.

- They are not able to come up with a Plan B.

How to help with flexibility difficulties

- Whenever possible, provide advance notice or warning of what's coming next – perhaps make time to look at your child's timetable together at the beginning of the day.

- Try to maintain schedules and routines whenever possible, while building in the possibility of flexibility – so try to discuss with your child the requirement to check their school email and school-based computer system during the day in case there are notifications about any changes in lessons / teachers. Sow the seed with your child that they need to be prepared for something like this if it happens.

- In general, help your child to anticipate what they might encounter in a situation – the more information they have in advance the more they will feel able to cope and navigate the unexpected.

- If you know what causes your child anxiety (a missed lesson or work notification etc.), walk them through the anxiety-producing situation, so you can talk about it and confront it, and come up with some strategies to manage it.

- Help your child come up with a few default strategies for handling situations where flexibility causes the most problems – this can include simple things like walking away from the situation for some cooling off time, and then returning and asking a specific person for help.

Use this checklist with your child, to help increase their awareness of what their possible triggers are:

Flexibility checklist

Flexibility difficulty	Yes / no	My comments
When I don't succeed the first time I tend to give up / find it hard to think of a new approach		

If plans or routines change I find it hard to adapt		
I have problems with open-ended classwork / homework assignments (e.g., I don't know what to write about / where to start)		

Here are some self-help strategies for your child.

Tips	Self-talk
Notice the physical warning signs of inflexibility (muscle tightness, breathing changes) and ask yourself if you can find a way to be flexible	Big deal or little deal?
Whenever you have to make a decision about something, ask yourself 'What could go wrong and what's Plan B if this doesn't work?'	What are your options? What is Plan B? Is there another way to think about this?
Other strategies:	Your own idea(s):

Guide 6: Task initiation

Task initiation is the ability to begin projects or activities without pro-crastination, in an efficient and timely manner. Using this skill can involve beginning a task as soon as it is assigned or deciding when a task will be done and beginning promptly at that predetermined time.

What you might see in your child if they have poor task initiation

- They do not know how to get started – they feel overwhelmed.
- They believe that the task will 'take forever'.
- They think they are not up to the job and so delay to avoid failure.
- They have difficulty re-engaging with a task after taking a break.
- They delay starting something because there are better / more interesting things to do first.

Children can often overestimate how much time they have to do a task in and underestimate how long the task will actually take. They will often also choose to complete an interesting or fun activity, both as a way to gain some immediate pleasure as well as a way of avoiding or escaping the non-preferred task.

How to help with task initiation difficulties

- Whenever possible use a work goal that your child has been encouraged to set themselves (rather than one imposed on them). However, if the goal / end result is far off in the future, or the number of tasks involved in achieving the goal is large, beginning the task may still be a problem.
- If a task seems overwhelming, encourage your child to work with you or their teacher to break the task down into more manageable parts, with specific deadlines for each part.
- Try to encourage them to make an explicit plan for when / how the task will get done. This will provide them more with ownership and control over the process, and can positively affect their ability to get started. Encouraging them to break the task down into small steps will make it seem more manageable.
- Where possible try to let your child decide on deadlines and cuing systems that work best for them in order to trigger a willingness to engage in task initiation.

- When the ball is rolling, keep it going; stopping and starting can be the enemy of task initiation, so if your child has successfully started on a task and they have the momentum and perseverance to be able to keep going, encourage them to do so, reminding them that it will get the job done more quickly and drag the task out less.

- Trying to stay positive will help with your child engaging more with task initiation.

Use this worksheet for your child to increase self-awareness of what their possible triggers are:

Worksheet: Increasing task initiation abilities (for non-preferred tasks)

Things I avoid	Yes / no	My comments
I find it hard to get started on homework		
I avoid things that will require effort or hard work		
I find other smaller tasks to do than starting a big project		
I find it hard to break tasks down into smaller chunks		
Anything else / your own ideas...		

Below are some self-help strategies for your child. Being able to make yourself start a task if you've seen yourself getting closer to your goal is the first step on that path. If you don't take this step, you cannot get closer.

Tips	Self-talk
Pick the task (make it small)	Just do it
Pick the start time	Take small steps
Pick the minimum work time	Start small
Pick the cue to start	
Other strategies:	**Your own idea(s):**

TWINK

- **T**hink about the task.
- **W**rite three steps to begin the task:

    - ....
    - ....
    - ....

- **I**nitiate (begin) the first step.
- **N**ext step – begin the next step.
- **K**eep on going.

Source: Taken from Moyes (2014, p.84)

Guide 7: Sustained attention

Sustained attention is the capacity to keep focusing on a situation or task in hand in spite of distractions, fatigue or boredom. This means being able to maintain attention in class, persevere with homework and complete any chores you set. If sustained attention is weak you will be conscious that your child may need directions / instructions to be repeated and that they are frequently off task. You may also be aware of your child jumping from one task to another and often failing to complete the preceding task before choosing to move on to a second. Your child may also look for distractions such as checking their phone every few minutes.

It should be noted that, as a generation, it is possible that our children have less capacity for sustained attention than previous generations, in part because of the fast-paced technological world in which they live, where things seem designed for instant gratification rather than sustained attention and perseverance.

Completing schoolwork at home can highlight difficulties with sustained attention, because your child will be working in isolation more often and will not have the external stimuli of classmates to help keep them motivated or against whom to compare their own ability to concentrate.

What you might see in your child if they have poor sustained attention

- They appear to be easily externally distracted by things in their environment, e.g., looking out of the window or being distracted by noises or activities going on around them.

- They are internally distracted, e.g., lost in their own thoughts.

- They need to take regular breaks when working.

- They find it hard to regulate the length of their breaks and therefore take breaks that are too long.

- They take breaks too frequently.

- They run out of steam before they have finished a task.

- They do not recognise for themselves when they are 'off task'.

How to help with sustained attention difficulties

- Try to encourage your child to identify particular tasks (e.g., homework) that are tough to focus on, and talk to them about whether there are ways to modify the tasks (such as breaking them into smaller parts) that would help them to maintain attention and complete the task.

- Provide supervision, by checking in with your child periodically to see how they are doing, or to help them put the distractions to one side.

- Try to have a discussion about how long your child feels they can work on a task before needing a break, and then discuss whether a timer would be a good idea to depict elapsed time (children can often have a distorted sense of the passage of time, particularly if it is a task they are reluctant to do).

- A regular very brief alarm / agreed upon cue can be effective to help your child refocus, if this sustained attention is a particular problem area for them.

- Use incentive systems, e.g., 'first...then' plans, whereby they complete the less preferred activity first and can then move on to a more preferred one.

- Always give praise for staying on task and for successfully completing a task (instead of negative connotations, such as your child perceiving that you nag them to get work done).

Here are some self-help strategies for you to encourage your child to do.

Tips	Self-talk
Set realistic work goals and stick to them	You cannot walk away from this
Take planned breaks and get back to work on schedule	Don't quit now
Gather all necessary materials before beginning a task	Back to work
Build in rewards for completing tasks	Work first, then play

Other strategies:	Your own idea(s):

TWINK

- **T**hink about the task.

- **W**rite three steps to begin the task:

  – ....

  – ....

  – ....

- **I**nitiate (begin) the first step.

- *Next step – begin the next step.*

- *Keep on going.*

Source: Taken from Moyes (2014, p.84)

Guide 8: Goal-directed persistence

Goal-directed persistence is the ability to set a goal and pursue its achievement. This skill requires your child to have an understanding that how they behave today has consequences that may impact later achievements.

What you might see in your child if they have poor goal-directed persistence

- They live in the 'now', with little awareness of future aspirations or consequences.
- They do not have an idea of what they want to achieve or where they want to go with their future plans.
- They find it hard to stick to a routine and follow something through.
- They do not complete things.

How you can support goal-directed persistence

- Promote practice and effort rather than outcome.
- Identify the importance of establishing a goal and carrying it through to completion.
- Help your child resist getting distracted by other interests.
- Encourage a growth mindset so that your child believes that their goals are attainable with application and some hard work.

GOAL PLANNING

List your goals:

....

....

Identify strategies to achieve them:

....

....

Set down the next steps:

....

....

Review

Did you complete the next steps?

What steps remain? [list them]

. . . .

. . . .

How can you be even more successful next time?

. . . .

. . . .

WORKSHEET: GETTING READY FOR LEARNING AND ACHIEVING MY GOALS

What are things in your workspace that you've noticed interfere with your concentration?

. . . .

. . . .

Is your workspace cluttered or organised?

. . . .

. . . .

What steps can you take to change your workspace for better concentration?

. . . .

. . . .

Break it down into a list:

. . . .

. . . .

Guide 9: Planning and prioritisation

Planning and prioritisation is the ability to create a set of steps to reach a goal or complete a task, coupled with the ability to focus on what is most important along the way.

When you have formulated a good plan, you know how to focus on what's most important and you know to let the little things go.

What you might see in your child who has poor planning and prioritisation

- They do not make a study plan (they don't know how).
- They are unable to break larger tasks into smaller ones with an order of achievement.
- They can't come up with timelines to complete things.
- They miss dates and deadlines.
- They do not have the foresight to take detailed notes to study from.
- They take too many notes and do not know how to detect important from unimportant facts.
- They spend too much time on less important elements – they find it difficult to put the most important jobs first.
- They are unrealistic about plans.

How to help with planning and prioritisation difficulties

- Encourage your child to plan, and include them as much as possible in the planning process for tasks that you might plan together.
- If your child appears to understand the various pieces of a project that need to get done but is not sure how to get started, prompt them to prioritise by asking what needs to get done as the first step, what the next step is, and so on in the process.

The following are some self-help strategies for you to encourage your child to do.

Tips	Self-talk
Create 'planning forms' to help keep you on track for bigger tasks	What's your destination?
Your plan will become a built-in satnav system to get there	Map the route
Work with classmates / friends / ask your teacher to help identify the most important points and concepts to focus on when studying for a test / producing a project	What comes first, next, next, and what do you need to give up to get there?
When you are given instructions for tasks and projects, underline and number each instruction so that it becomes an action to be completed	First things first
Other strategies:	Your own idea(s):

Here are some examples of different types of study plans.

Identifying tasks and due dates

What do I need to do? (List each step in order)	When will I do it?	Check off when done
1.		
2.		
3.		
4.		

Reminder list

Include any additional tasks or details you need to keep in mind as you work. Cross out or check each one off as you do it

1.

2.

3.

4.

5.

6.

7.

Daily reminders – things I cannot forget

Monday	Tuesday	Wednesday	Thursday	Friday	Saturday	Sunday

Guide 10: Organisation

Organisation is the ability to create and maintain a system for arranging and keeping track of important things.

Keeping track of things and having a reasonably organised bedroom and work environment increases efficiency by eliminating the need to waste lots of time looking for things – it is important to quickly get ready to work on a task or project. This, in turn, reduces stress.

If your child has a tendency to overestimate how much time they have and to underestimate how much time a task will take (see Guide 5), they may be operating quite close to the edge to begin with, and not being able to find essential materials is an unnecessary and avoidable stress that might prevent them collapsing into difficulties.

What you might see in a pupil who has poor organisational skills

- They have a messy, poorly organised school bag.

- They have a messy, poorly organised bedroom.

- They lose things or forget where they have been left.

- They do not know how to organise / set out a written piece of work.

- They do not know how to save electronic work in a logical manner with an effective filing system.

How to help with organisation difficulties

- To help your child develop organisational skills it is best to approach it from an area that they have an investment in.

- In the short term offer your child reminders (that they can tolerate) about their organisation, even though your goal is to be able to withdraw those reminders in due course.

- Offering to help your child clean and organise their space from time to time can be helpful.

- Where possible try to model some simple organisational operations for your child. Try to share examples from your own life.

What good organisational skills will look like

- A tidy desk and bedroom so they can find things when they need them.

- Making numbers and calculations orderly and easy to follow in maths, well set out science and geographical formulae, diagrams etc.

- Being able to write essays and longer answers so that their ideas on one topic are all in one section or paragraph.

Self-help strategies for you to encourage your child to do

- Have a system to store schoolwork – in folders or books depending on your teachers' preferences.

- Use an organiser – write a note about INCOMPLETE WORK in it and also record any tasks that you are set, as soon as they are set; also note the due date for all work.

- Write the DUE DATE for tasks that are set on the top of the task sheet itself, as soon as you get it, so that there is a visible reminder about when it should be done by.

- As soon as you finish an assignment, mark it off as completed in your organiser, and file the completed work away.

- Keep all your work filed away properly. Throw out pieces of paper that you do not have to keep – check with the teacher if you are unsure.

- Have / develop a system for keeping your work materials (such as pens, pencils, erasers, calculators etc.) tidy.

- If you are creative you can make yourself useful 'organisers' from household recycling – cleaned-out tins for different items of stationery like colouring pens, pencils, rulers etc.; creating organisers / planners, using colour coding to help organise books by subject; covered cereal boxes with a large side removed as a 'to do' box / filing system.

- Try to remove unnecessary items or clutter from your room / workspace.

- Anticipate what you will need to get ready for school by getting things prepared and ready the night before – pack bags, make sure clothes are ready etc.

- Use memory aids (visual aids / checklists).

- Try to observe what organised people do...

ESSAY WRITING TEMPLATE

Introductory paragraph

Sentence 1 sets out what your essay is going to be about.

Sentence 2 details the main point you want to make during your essay.

Sentence 3 expands on this and / or identifies why the topic is an important one.

Main body of the essay – the paragraphs

Paragraph 1: Introductory topic sentence – the point / focus of the paragraph.

What is the evidence to support this point? Provide an explanation about the point you are making.

Paragraph 2: Introductory topic sentence – the point / focus of the paragraph.

What is the evidence to support this point? Provide an explanation about the point you are making.

Paragraph 3: Introductory topic sentence – the point / focus of the paragraph.

What is the evidence to support this point? Provide an explanation about the point you are making.

Concluding paragraph

Refer back to your introduction – what was your most important point? Re-state it here, drawing your argument to a close.

Guide 11: Time management

Time management is affected by other EF skills – task initiation, sustained attention, planning and prioritisation, and organisation. The most common misconception among children and teenagers is how long something might take to do and therefore underestimating the amount of time needed, thereby not planning and organising themselves effectively, and not initiating tasks in a timely manner. Sometimes, conversely, they will overestimate how long something will take and this can then make the task seem overwhelming, and so it becomes difficult to start, thereby making task initiation planning and prioritisation and organisation skills trickier to manage.

Time estimation can be improved through practice, and so a good habit to get into is encouraging your child to estimate how long they *think* a task will take and then comparing it to how long it actually *does* take. This can help your child to improve their concept of time.

What you might see in a child who has poor time management skills

- They have difficulty estimating how long a task will take – due to:
  - Overestimating how long it will take to do a task (therefore never getting started).
  - Underestimating how long it will take to do a task (therefore running out of time).
- They are chronically late getting ready for school / obligations / appointments.
- They have difficulty juggling multiple tasks and responsibilities because they are not managing their time properly.
- They lack a sense of urgency / do not appreciate that deadlines are important.
- They rely on a deadline as an activator and motivator (and leave things to the last minute in order to feel motivated by a very short deadline to complete things).

How to help with time management difficulties

- Try to encourage your child to stick to a routine, particularly for studying, but also for sleep and other daily routines.

- Encourage your child to make a commitment with you to follow a schedule. You may put this on the fridge or another obvious place as a reminder. You may also need (initially) to give your child reminders when the time comes to do something.

- Encourage your child to set alarms or use apps or programs on phones etc., to help them get started on time. Pomodoro is an app that can help with breaking tasks into segments; other apps are also available.

- Encourage your child to create checklists and 'to do' lists and an estimation of how long tasks will take.

Below are some self-help strategies for you to encourage your child to do. Good time management allows you to manage the different demands of what you want to do, what you need to do, and what others ask you to do.

Tips	Self-talk
Use a planner to make daily plans	How much time do you have?
Estimate how long a task will last – and then check to see if you were right	Are you on track?
Break work / homework down into short time segments	What you need to do comes before what you *want* to do
	Honestly, how long will it really take?
Other strategies:	**Your own idea(s):**

Other strategies:	Your own idea(s):

Weekly planner
(Adapt lesson times to suit your own school day.)

Week: [add date]	Monday	Tuesday	Wednesday	Thursday	Friday
Period 1 9.00–9.55					
Period 2 9.55–10.50					
Period 3 11.15–12.10					
Period 4 12.10–13.05					
Period 5 14.05–15.00					
Period 6 15.00–15.55					

Fill in your weekly planner; you could colour-code your lessons to help it to be more visual.

Tasks to be accomplished this week
Add the tasks you have been set, and when they are due.

Here is an example of a half-termly planner.

Monday	Tuesday	Wednesday	Thursday	Friday	Saturday	Sunday
4th	5th	6th	7th	8th	9th	10th
11th	12th	13th	14th	15th	16th	17th
18th	19th	20th	21st	22nd	HALF TERM	HALF TERM

Guide 12: Working memory

Working memory is the ability to store information for a limited amount of time and to do something with the information, for example to apply it to a task.

What you might see in a child who has a poor working memory

- Forgetfulness – they forget to take necessary kit into school, to bring necessary kit home, and do not have the correct materials needed for class / home.

- They forget to record homework properly, missing deadlines, and do not hand in homework on time.

- They forget due dates for longer-term projects or tests, and miss deadlines.

- They lose their train of thought.

- They have difficulty following instructions, particularly if there are multiple steps.

- They lose things or forget where they have been left.

How to help with working memory difficulties

- Try to make eye contact with your child before telling them something you want them to remember.

- Try to avoid external distractions when giving your child directions.

- If you are not sure whether your child has really heard / listened to you, ask them to paraphrase what you have said back to you.

- Use written reminders – lists, Post-it® notes, calendars etc.

- Encourage your child to use technological solutions to aid working memory by setting reminders of specific events etc. (such as apps, smartphones and digital calendars)

- When your child is going to be involved in an activity or task that they have had experience of before, reinforce their prior successes as a way of reminding them to draw on their past experiences.

- Encourage your child to 'teach you' (e.g., get them to practise explaining a skill or activity) – this helps them to remember all the steps needed to complete the task.

- Play games that use visual memory (Pairs, Kim's Game, I Spy, puzzles, spot the difference).

- Play card games (Crazy Eights, Uno, Go Fish etc.)

- Regularly complete Sudoku puzzles, crosswords etc.

- Practise active reading strategies (taking notes, using sticky notes, asking questions as they are reading etc.).

Guide 13: Metacognition

Metacognition refers to the ability to stand back and observe yourself from the outside, that is, how you problem solve and decide what is called for in a given situation. When you have this skill, you can make decisions about how to proceed based on what you understand about yourself. While doing this you ask yourself 'How am I doing?' Then evaluate how you did, and decide how to do things differently in the future.

Metacognition is a skill based on a combination of understanding your own behaviour and past experiences, as well as monitoring your behaviour as you adjust to some current new situation.

What you might see in a child who has poor metacognitive awareness

- They cannot accurately evaluate skills (e.g., expecting to do well in tests, despite poor past performance / preparation).

- They cannot identify appropriate study strategies.

- They cannot plan or organise a written piece of work.

- They can memorise facts but miss the larger context (they do better on multiple choice tests than essay questions).

- They do not proofread their work.

- They do not know what to study.

- They do not know how to study.

How to help with metacognition difficulties

- Provide specific praise for task performance, by recognising strategies that your child uses, e.g., for chores, performance on schoolwork, interactions with friends etc. Provide specific praise such as 'you're good at understanding your friends' feelings'.

- Encourage your child to evaluate their own performance on a task or in a social situation.

- Encourage your child to ask teachers for feedback as a way to improve performance.

- Use your behaviour as a way of indirectly helping your child understand how people might react to their behaviour.

Here are some self-help strategies for you to encourage your child to do.

Tips	Self-talk
Ask teachers for revision sheets for tests	What's the big picture?
Create your own study packs for tests by pulling together all important material, amalgamating and condensing your notes	How are you doing?
Create self-monitoring checklists (e.g., a proofreading checklist)	What worked for you before?
Ask yourself four self-monitoring questions: What is my problem? What is my plan? Am I following my plan? How did I do?	What didn't work?
	What do you need or want for a grade?
	Have you studied enough to get it?
Other strategies:	**Your own idea(s):**

Proofreading checklist

- Do all sentences begin with a capital letter?

- Have all proper nouns got capital letters?

- Are all sentences complete sentences?

- Did I use appropriate paragraphs, with one key idea per paragraph?

- Do all sentences have ending punctuation? (. ! ?)

- Did I use commas and quotation marks correctly?

- Did I spell every word correctly?

Three-colour highlighting

- Main points (often the first or last paragraph in a section or the first sentence in a paragraph).

- Supporting details (elaborating on the main points, provides evidence or proof to support assertions or opinions).

- Terms (key vocabulary or concepts).

Bibliography

Baddeley, A. (1996) 'Exploring the central executive.' *Quarterly Journal of Experimental Psychology 49*, 1. https://doi.org/10.1080/713755608

Baddeley, A. D. and Hitch, G. (1974) 'Working memory.' *Psychology of Learning and Motivation 8*, 47–89. https://doi.org/10.1016/S0079-7421(08)60452-1

Baker, L. and Brown, A. L. (1984) 'Metacognitive Skills and Reading.' In P. D. Pearson (Ed.), *Handbook of Reading Research* (pp.353–394). New York: Longman.

Cooper-Kahn, M. and Foster, M. (2013) *Boosting Executive Skills in the Classroom: A Practical Guide for Educators.* San Francisco, CA: Jossey-Bass.

Department for Education (2023) *Special Educational Needs Disability: An Analysis and Summary of Data Sources.* June. https://assets.publishing.service.gov.uk/media/64930eef103ca6001303a3a6/Special_educational_needs_and_disability_an_analysis_and_summary_of_data_sources.pdf

Diamond, A. and Lee, K. (2011) 'Interventions shown to aid executive function development in children 4 to 12 years old.' *Science (American Association for the Advancement of Science) 333*, 6045, 959–964. https://doi.org/10.1126/science.1204529

Dweck, C. S. (2017) *Mindset: Changing the Way You Think to Fulfil Your Potential* (Revised Edn). London: Robinson.

Ebbinghaus, H. (1885 [1962]) *Memory: A Contribution to Experimental Psychology.* New York: Dover.

Faith, L., Bush, C. and Dawson, P. (2022) *Executive Function Skills in the Classroom.* New York: Guilford Press.

Flavell, J. H. (1979) 'Metacognition and cognitive monitoring: A new area of cognitive-developmental inquiry.' *American Scientist 34*, 906–911.

Goldrich, C. and Goldrich, C. (2019) *ADHD Executive Function & Behavioural Challenges in the Classroom.* Wisconsin: PESI Publishing & Media.

Guare, R., Dawson, P. and Guare, C. (2009) *Smart But Scattered: The Revolutionary 'Executive Skills' Approach to Helping Kids Reach Their Potential.* New York: The Guilford Press.

Guare, R., Dawson, P. and Guare, C. (2013) *Smart But Scattered Teens: The 'Executive Skills' Program for Helping Teens Reach Their Potential.* New York: The Guilford Press.

Koschnitzky, J. (2015) 'Neurons – a brain superhighway!' Hydrocephalus Association Blog, 15 January. www.hydroassoc.org/neurons-a-brain-superhighway

Locascio, G., Mahone, E. M., Eason, S. H. and Cutting, L. E. (2010) 'Executive dysfunction among children with reading comprehension deficits.' *Journal of Learning Disabilities 43*, 5, 441–454. https://doi.org/10.1177/0022219409355476

Meltzer, L. (2010) *Promoting Executive Function in the Classroom*. What Works for Special Needs Learners. New York: Guilford Press.

Miyake, A. and Friedman, N. P. (2012) 'The nature and organization of individual differences in executive functions: Four general conclusions.' *Current Directions in Psychological Science 21*, 1, 8–14. https://doi.org/10.1177/0963721411429458

Moyes, R. A. (2014) *Executive Function 'Dysfunction': Strategies for Educators and Parents*. London: Jessica Kingsley Publishers.

Naglieri, J. A. (2005). The Cognitive Assessment System. In D. P. Flanagan & P. L. Harrison (Eds.), *Contemporary Intellectual Assessment: Theories, Tests, and Issues* (pp. 441 -460). New York: The Guilford Press.

Siegel, D. J. (2001) 'Toward an interpersonal neurobiology of the developing mind: Attachment relationships, "mindsight," and neural integration.' *Infant Mental Health Journal 22*, 1–2, 67–94. https://doi.org/10.1002/1097-0355(200101/04)22:1<67::AID-IMHJ3>3.0.CO;2-G

Toll, S. W. M., van der Ven, S. H., Kroesbergen, E. and van Luit, J. E. (2011) 'Executive functions as predictors of math learning disabilities.' *Journal of Learning Disabilities 44*, 6, 521–532. https://doi.org/10.1177/0022219410387302

Tuckman, A. (2012) *Understand Your Brain, Get More Done: The AHDS Executive Functions Workbook*. Plantation, FL: Speciality Press, Inc.

Willingham, D. T. (2005–06) 'Ask the cognitive scientist: How praise can motivate – or stifle.' Education Healthcare Public Services, America Educator, Winter. www.aft.org/ae/winter2005-2006/willingham

Zelazo, P. D., Blair, C. B. and Willoughby, M. T. (2016) *Executive Function: Implications for Education* (NCER 2017-2000). Washington, DC: National Center for Education Research, Institute of Education Sciences, U.S. Department of Education. http://ies.ed.gov